GARY E. TUCK

Abigail Adams wrote:

—On her husband's election to the Presidency:

"And now, O Lord, My God, Thou hast made Thy servant ruler over the people. Give unto him an understanding heart that he may know how to go out and come in before this great people; that he may discern between good and bad . . ."

—On politics:

"That cannot be politically right which is morally wrong."

—On the need for Christian society:

"I am no friend of bigotry, yet I think the freedom of inquiry, and the general toleration of religious sentiments, have been, like all other good things, perverted, and, under their shelter, deism, and even atheism, have found refuge."

—On the issue of slavery:

"I have sometimes been ready to think that the passion for Liberty cannot be equally strong in the breasts of those who have been accustomed to deprive their fellow Creatures of theirs. Of this I am certain that it (slavery) is not founded upon that generous and Christian principle of doing to others as we would that others should do unto us."

—On living the Christian life:

"The race is not to the swift, nor the battle to the strong, but the God of Israel is he that giveth strength and power unto His people."

D0904017

Copper Works

Bartons Point

Charles River

Rope Walk

Rope Walk

Lee's Ship Yard

Eb.N. Mill Damm

Ferry to Charles Town

N. Water Mill

Lees Ship Yd

Hudsons Point

Hunt & Whites Ship Yd

Mill Pond

Ferry W.

Burying Place

Bakers

Boling Green

Baptist Meeting

Salem Street

Water Mill

Bartons Yard.

Hanover

Back Street

North Street

Middle Street

N. Battery

Burroughs W.

Green & Greenwood Ship & Wharf.

Charks Ship Yd

Hutchinson's W.

Ship Street

Cornhill

King Street

Lees Ship Yd

Clarks W.

Old Wharfe.

Scarletts Wharfe.

Clarks Wharf.

Woodmans Wharf.

Bundls W.

Wentworths Wharfe

Long Wharfe

Old Wharfe.

Cools Whar.

Olivers Docks

Farmers W.

Greenleafs W.

Longs Wharf

Wings shy'd

Olivers Wharfe

Old Wharfe

Fort Hill

S Battery.

Hubbards W.

Graham W.

HARBOUR

ng. Boston N E. 1722.   Sold by Capt. John Bonner And Willm Price against ÿ Town House where may be had all sorts of Prints Mappse

Dedicated

To my dear daughter, Louise.

FIRST LADY OF FAITH AND COURAGE

ABIGAIL ADAMS

by Evelyn Witter
edited by Norma Cournow Camp

illustrated by
Linda Crockett-Hanzel

Mott Media

MILFORD, MICHIGAN 48042

All Scriptures are from the King James Version of the Bible.

COPYRIGHT © 1976 by Mott Media
Second Printing, 1981

All rights in this book are reserved. No portion of this book may be reproduced by any process such as mimeograph, photocopying, recording, storage in a retrieval or transmitted by any means without written permission of the publisher. Brief quotations embodied in critical article or reviews are permitted. For information write Mott Media, 1000 East Huron, Milford, Michigan 48042.

All Rights Reserved

Robert F. Burkett, Editor

LIBRARY OF CONGRESS CATALOGING IN PUBLICATION DATA

Witter, Evelyn.
  Abigail Adams, first lady of faith and courage.

  (The Sowers)
  Bibliography: p. 141
  Includes index.

  SUMMARY: Abigail Adams relates the story of her life from childhood to the end of her husband's term as second President of the United States.
  1. Adams, Abigail Smith, 1744-1818—Juvenile literature. (1. Adams, Abigail Smith, 1744-1818. 2. Presidents—wives) I. Title.

E322.1.A38W57   1976   973.4'4'0924 (b) (92) 76-2416
ISBN 0-915134-08-X

CONTENTS

Page

Foreword   ix
Chapter I
   Happy Birthday! 1
Chapter II
   Explosion! 16
Chapter III
   At Grandmother Quincy's 30
Chapter IV
   Boisterous Boston 43
Chapter V
   John Adams 52
Chapter VI
   Mrs. John Adams 64
Chapter VII
   Happenings In Boston 74
Chapter VIII
   Pewter And Bullets 85
Chapter IX
   Independence 96
Chapter X
   Citizen Of The World 105
Chapter XI
   The Vice-President's Lady 117
Chapter XII
   First Lady 130
Bibliography 141
Index 142

FOREWORD

Now and then in the recorded history of America a person comes on the scene who remains for all times an inspiration to Christians. Such a woman was Abigail Adams.

A born-again Christian, her whole life was guided by His Word. She was steadfast through fortune and misfortune.

As the second First Lady she was President John Adams' partner. Many of her precepts helped guide and mold America. Her own son, John Quincy Adams, who she trained up in God's Word was our sixth President.

Her relationships with the people of her world, her letters, and her acts of faith and courage, have come down to us as an important part of our heritage.

Evelyn Witter

Chapter I

Happy Birthday!

It was the magical day of November 18, 1749. My fifth birthday and Grandmother Quincy was coming from Mount Wollaston! You can be sure, I was excited. It wasn't only the trunk of presents Grandmother Quincy would bring that excited me, even if my seven-year-old sister, Mary, said it was. What excited me most was the way Grandmother always told the story of my birth. I never tired of hearing about the Indians, tomahawk, and snowstorm.

I ran impatiently from one window to the next, squinting hardest at the north window. I knew Grandmother would come from

Mount Wollaston to the north of us.

"Be patient." My father, Reverend William Smith, smiled at me as he threw another log into the fireplace. "Grandmother and Grandfather will come. As it says in Ecclesiastes 'The patient in spirit is better than the proud in spirit.'"

But it was hard to have patience and be excited too. Now the snow began to fall giving me a new worry. In Weymouth, Massachusetts, storms were often big, keeping people in their homes for days.

Snowflakes hit the windowpane. Snow already covered the ground, and now with the coming of more snow, Grandmother and Grandfather would surely have to come by sleigh.

Then Tom, our hired man called out, "They're here! They're here!"

I heard the welcomed crunch of the sleigh runners on the snow and the steady rhythm of the horses' hoofs as they drew near. The horses' breath hung on the air as puffs of white haze. Grandfather Quincy hoisted Grandmother down and they hurried toward the house.

"Grandmother! Grandfather!" I shouted, and soon they were hugging me and their kisses dampened my lips and cheeks. Mother and Father helped hang their great coats in the closet. Phoebe, our hired girl, served hot tea beside the fire, and quickly took away the foot warmers Tom brought in from the sleigh. My sister Mary and I sat quietly but impatiently waiting for present time. The grown-ups talked and talked. We smiled knowingly as my younger brother, Will, saw his chance to grab a quince tart from the tea table. Mother whacked his hand and he sat scowling in the corner. Will was never careful about his manners.

"Oh!" escaped from my lips as Tom brought in Grandmother's trunk. I crossed in front of the hearth to stand as close as possible to it.

The fire was sending flickering lights which reflected off the lemon-colored satin curtains. My eyes traced the patterns on the thick Brussels carpet with green leaves and lemon-colored flowers. I thought I'd burst if I didn't soon see the gifts. As I looked at the grown-ups, I smiled. It was my birthday and my aunts and grandparents were gathered here to celebrate with me! "How great are my blessings!" I thought.

Grandmother interrupted my dreaming with, "Nabby, bring the shawl I left on my last visit. It's in your room, I believe."

I wanted to run for the shawl, but I knew Grandmother would say running wasn't ladylike. I moved quickly none-the-less because the sooner I got the shawl the sooner I would get my presents and hear Grandmother tell the story.

But I forgot about being ladylike when I came down the stairs my special way. I went down one, two, three stairs quickly, then paused on the fourth. I took the fifth, sixth, and seventh stairs very fast, and then on the count of eight I took a little bounce that landed me right on the entry floor.

Father watched me with his large brown eyes. He was sitting very stiffly, his wide shoulders hunched a bit the same way they did when he plowed.

"Abigail," Mother said, "I told you not to

come down the stairs like that. Why—why it's like dancing."

"I know," I said, "and a clergyman's daughter isn't supposed to dance. It's really not dancing, Father. It's just the way I walk sometimes."

"I know," Father said gently.

"Now, child," said Grandmother Quincy, drawing the shawl about her slim shoulders, "here is the key. When you have received your other gifts, you may open the trunk. There are some things in it for your birthday."

At that moment, Mother, Mary and Will put something into my hand.

"Two bayberry candles for my room!" I exclaimed. Mary and Will knew how much I appreciated the sweet bayberry's scent after the homemade, smoky, greasy-smelling candles made of tallow and other animal fats.

"Thank you!" I said. My sister and brother saw by my happy face how much they had pleased me and grinned back at me.

Then Phoebe, her black face glowing, took something from her apron pocket — two maple sugar confections. Phoebe had made them herself, and no one could make maple confections like Phoebe.

"Happy birthday, Miss Nabby!" Phoebe smiled.

I hugged dear Phoebe and told her these would be saved to nibble on later.

Aunt Mary reached behind her. "These three aprons are from your three aunts, dear," she said.

"They'll save my good clothes while I chore," I said.

"Yes, indeed," said Aunt Anne. Aunt Elizabeth nodded in agreement.

"Now," Mother said, reaching for a box beside her chair, "here is something you've been waiting for a long time."

I opened the lid and there lay a white fur muff. "How beautiful it is, Mother!" I exclaimed. "Oh, thank you, thank you!" I pushed my hands inside the muff and felt its softness and warmth. "No more cold hands at Sunday services," I said.

Then Father moved beside me. "Nabby," he said, "what I have in my waistcoat pocket was made by a good friend of ours. He's a fine silversmith who lives in Boston named Paul Revere. He has fashioned this for you."

Father took an object from his waistcoat pocket and placed it in my hand. It was a silver ink well with simple lines and fine engraving.

"I shall treasure it forever, Father," I said.

"And use it daily," Father added with that schoolmaster look he sometimes gave me.

"It is time to open the trunk," Grandmother Quincy said.

My fingers trembled turning the key and

lifting the lid. There on top was a blue dress with crewelwork trim.

"Oh, Grandmother!" I cried. "It's lovely!"

I gave the dress to Mother to admire and pass around the circle of relatives while I dug deeper into the trunk. There were books, books, and more books.

"They came on the *Gildeon* from England," Grandfather explained.

I was glad to have books. Since I was thought to be too delicate to go to school, Father taught me at home. I spent much time in Father's study. I liked it there. The shelves were full of books. Of course, I couldn't read many of them yet, but I was learning. I read Scripture. Well, not exactly, but I had heard certain passages so often that I could guess at most of the words. Father first began teaching me my letters and numbers when I was four. Today I was five and could really read.

At first Father used the *Hornbook* which was made up of pages from the *New England Primer*. It was covered with thin, clear sheets of horn. In less than a year I could read parts of the catechism and some of the hymns in the *Bay Psalm Book*.

Once I heard Father tell Mother, "She's the smartest child in Weymouth."

Mother said, "Abigail learns easily, yes, but she is too delicate to walk the two miles across the fields to the Dame's School as Mary does."

"Then," said Father, "I'll continue teaching her at home."

I hardly had time to look at all my books from Grandmother when Mother said, "It's time for dinner. We're having maple sugar for the corn pudding, Nabby, in honor of your birthday."

Father said especially long prayers for the occasion. I tried to listen to every word, but my mind kept slipping into thoughts of the great story of my birth we would hear after dinner.

Corn pudding was always the first course in our house as it was in most New England households.

Father took his time carving the chicken. Today Phoebe seemed especially slow bringing in the biscuits and milk. And then the men started talking about the Molasses Act of 1733 and about a French expedition which was now on the Ohio River burying lead plates ever so often marking where they thought the French Territory was. Father said an English company of Virginian planters, with a royal patent, was surveying the same territory.

Suddenly Father jumped to his feet crying, "God save the king!"

That salute to George II usually ended political discussions. Today I was especially grateful to hear it. I wanted to listen to Grandmother Quincy talk about me.

I soon got my wish. Everyone moved back to the sitting room, and Mother said, "How well I remember this date five years ago!"

"Yes," said Grandmother, "five years ago today our dear Abigail was born. What a memorable day that was!"

I took the footstool and sat next to Grandmother, my elbow resting on her knee. I looked up into the pleasant face framed by her prettiest lace cap.

"Tell us, Grandmother," I said, settling comfortably on the stool.

"Should I start with the Indians?" Grandmother asked.

"No," giggled Mary, "please start at the beginning."

Grandmother looked affectionately from one to the other of the group, but her eyes rested on me at last and from then on I had the feeling that she was talking mostly to me. She petted the top of my head with her soft, white hand and the silk of her dress rustled deliciously.

Grandmother began, "It was a fearful night. The snow was so thick that the houses were solid white. The wind whipped and whistled with the fierceness of a gale at sea. There was no sign of life anywhere in Weymouth except right here in this house. Candles burned in every room and no one complained even though they knew the precious candle supply was fast disappearing.

"Abigail, you were born that night, but you were extremely tiny. After a few days we decided to send an Indian runner to get Grandfather Quincy. We decided the baby was too small and too delicate to survive. He must come before we lost her.

"Reverend Smith thought the baby didn't look any worse than she had. But even he wasn't sure about her condition. I didn't express what I thought," Grandmother shook her head knowingly.

"Aunt Elizabeth went downstairs to Aunt Mary and Aunt Anne and told them that we all felt the baby was too delicate to live much longer.

"'The little thing is about the same,' Aunt Elizabeth told the other aunts. 'It's well that the Indian runner went after Grandfather Quincy. I doubt if she will live another day.'

"Then, by the time light was breaking, Reverend Smith sent Tom out to the barn to hitch up a horse. Tom began clearing the road between the parsonage and meeting-house by dragging a heavy log over it.

"People looked out their houses. They didn't think anyone would be going to the parsonage this day. They were curious.

"'What are you doing, Tom?' they called out.

"'Clearing the way for Reverend Smith and his family,' Tom called back to them. 'Reverend Smith is going to baptize his baby daughter today. She's very sickly and not likely to live. The mother wants her to have a name, so they are going ahead with the christening, weather or not . . .'"

Grandmother Quincy paused. She stroked my hair lovingly.

Then Grandmother went on with the story. "It seemed like just a few minutes after Tom cleared the road that people began coming. They brought potions of every kind. Some were made with boiled snails, or worms, or even more loathsome ingredients. They smelled spoiled and offended the nose. I did give the baby a tiny taste, and she screamed at the top of her lungs.

"The three aunts were kept busy answering the door. I wanted to assist them, but Abigail cried when I tried to put her back in her cradle. So many people came that even little Mary helped by running to the door and letting people in.

"I did not know what to do with all the medicine people brought. Each person was sure her medicine would be best for the baby. But, Abigail didn't want any of it."

"It was nice of people to show so much concern," Mother said.

"Everyone loved Reverend Smith and his wife even as they do now," Aunt Anne spoke up for the first time.

Grandmother continued. "The Reverend decided to hurry on with the christening, but my daughter, the baby's mother, wanted to wait for her father.

"Aunt Mary didn't think waiting was wise. She was sure he couldn't get through because one could not see the road. It was completely covered over with snow.

"I told them, 'A snow storm won't stop my husband. Colonel John Quincy will be here.'

"It was the strangest thing. No sooner had I made that statement than we heard shouts outside. When I looked out I saw Colonel Quincy and two other people, all on horseback, coming toward the house. When they got closer I could see the two riders with him were Indians. One was the chief of the Ponkapoag Indians and the other was the Indian runner, Robert, who had gone to bring the Colonel. The Indians had come to honor the granddaughter of their friend."

"Did you take me downstairs to see the Indians?" I asked. I knew the answer, but somehow Grandmother always expected me to ask at this part of the story.

"Not immediately," smiled Grandmother. "We had to dress you for the christening first."

"What did Abigail wear?" Mary asked.

This was the part Grandmother seemed to enjoy the most and we knew it.

Grandmother settled back in her chair and looked straight ahead as if seeing the scene all over again. Then she began counting on her fingers as she spoke, "There were stacks of long petticoats trimmed with lace and embroidery. There was the dress of the finest cambric that I had had made for the baby's mother when she was christened. Then there was that elegant hood and a silk jacket and several white, woolen blankets. You were then taken downstairs, Abigail.

"Everyone looked at the baby and they all remarked how sweet she was, but there was a sadness all around. Everyone was thinking the baby would never grow much bigger. This little angel would never live to run, play, skip and hop, they thought.

"It was then Grandfather Quincy got his first look at his granddaughter, Abigail. He said, 'I thought you said the baby was thin. She's fat.'

"That remark of the Colonel's broke through some of the gloom. Actually, the baby did look fat because she had on so many clothes. In fact, she looked like a fat, little featherbed.

"It was then my husband said, 'She'll be all right. We'll be proud of her someday.' He turned to the Indian chief and asked, 'What do you think, Chief Mummentaug?'

"I walked right over to the chief and laid Abigail in his arms. The chief studied the baby for a while and then he said, 'She's little, but she'll live to be a great lady like her grandmother.'"

"Wasn't that a nice thing for him to say!" I exclaimed as I always did at this part of the story.

"Yes," smiled Mother, "and when he gave my baby back to my mother, he gave her a doeskin robe the Indian women had made."

Grandmother went on. "Tom came in at that moment and whispered to me that it was getting colder and that it would be best if we got on with it.

"When we got outside the icy wind grabbed our breaths right out of our bodies. I led the way with Abigail in my arms. Neighbors joined us, and when we reached the meetinghouse almost all of Weymouth was with us.

"Of course as we walked along I had no

idea how the baby was under the robe. I couldn't feel her stirring. Once inside the meetinghouse, when I lifted the robe, I was so relieved. The darling little thing was sound asleep.

"The Reverend Smith hastened into the baptismal ceremony. But when he went to the baptismal font, the water was frozen.

"There was no heat in the meetinghouse, and he was afraid the baby would suffer bad effects from the cold. He was anxious to have the ceremony over quickly. Reverend Smith hit the ice on the font with his fist, but it didn't break.

"The old Indian Chief saw the trouble. He reached inside his robe, drew out a tomahawk and gave it to Reverend Smith. With one tomahawk whack the ice broke and the ceremony proceeded.

"I named the baby Abigail for the Reverend Smith's mother."

"I'm glad you named me Abigail after father's mother," I said.

Grandmother patted my hand and went on with her story. "We hurried back to the house. Phoebe had roasted turkeys, chickens, geese, beef, and ham ready. The pantry shelves were filled with custards, puddings, pies, and cakes too. In the big brick oven next to the open fireplace, pans of corn bread smelled delicious.

"Reverend Smith was grateful for this day and before we ate he offered a beautiful prayer of heartfelt thankfulness. Then he wrote in the church record."

"May I show that entry?" Father asked reaching for the record book.

He opened it to the page where he had written:

I baptized my daughter today, November 25, 1744.

Everyone looked at the entry and nodded their approval.

"When you wrote that about Abigail, I asked you what you were writing, didn't I, Father?" Mary asked.

"Yes," smiled Father. "I told you then that the baby's name was Abigail."

"Yes," Mary smiled back, "and I hurried over to my aunts to tell them the name. When they asked me what it was, I told them 'Nabby.'"

"That was as close as you could get to Abigail. Before long everyone was calling Abigail 'Nabby,'" Father added to the story.

Grandmother Quincy took up the story again. "For weeks people stopped in to see how the baby was. They wanted to look at her and to give their advice. They always went away shaking their heads. Some said, 'Be prepared. It looks as if she isn't long for this world.'"

"But they were all wrong," Grandfather Quincy cut in. "She did live as I told them from the first that she would."

Then everyone clapped and I made a curtsy and the children were allowed to run into the kitchen to play. That was a happy day. But not far ahead, dark clouds were to hang over the Smith household because of a fire in Weymouth that could be seen many miles away in Boston.

Chapter II

𝕰𝖝𝖕𝖑𝖔𝖘𝖎𝖔𝖓!

It was a sweet April day when I discovered a secret about the meetinghouse. Nature was coming awake for the summer and every day new growths were springing out. The trees were pushing out their first burst of tender green. I could see buttercups nodding in the breeze near the meetinghouse, and there were early violets blooming at the edge of the woods.

On this April Saturday Father and Will strolled up to the meetinghouse to talk with Sam, the church sexton who took care of the building. Mary and I started the stroll with them, but we were stopped by Mrs. Trudy who always asked too many questions and Mrs. Pratt who lived far up on a hill nearby. Father and Will were at the meetinghouse long before we finished our visits.

As we skipped along I could still hear Mother's remarks to Phoebe that very morning and I did try to be more ladylike.

Mother had said, "I'm glad Abigail is so friendly, but have you noticed how undignified she is? She runs and strides like a boy. We can't have that. I've been so concerned with her health, I fear I have neglected her manners."

"She's the friendliest girl in Massachusetts," Phoebe had answered, "always looking out for other people. She's Christian, Mistress Smith. She's a good Christian girl."

We got to the meetinghouse when Father was saying to Sam, "I must take a look at the garret."

Father went inside and up the stairs to the balcony. He went straight to the door that led to the garret. His hands rubbed along the molding until he found a key.

I started to follow him, but he turned quickly and said, "No, Abigail. You must wait here with Mary and Will. I can't allow children in the garret."

"Why not?" I asked.

Father was already out of sight. Sam rubbed his chin as if considering whether to answer me or not. He decided to tell me why because he said, "The town's supply of gunpowder is up there. We have three barrels of it. It could blow us all to glory. No place for children."

Mary began to bite her lip and wriggle like she always does when she's nervous. "What is our father doing up in the garret with all that gunpowder?" she asked.

"Well," explained Sam, scratching his head, "since he's the pastor here at Weymouth he's thought to be responsible for the whole town. You see what I mean, Miss?

Being responsible the way he is he wants to
make sure the gunpowder's dry. He'll be sure
to look over the rifles too to make sure they'll
be ready in case we need them."

Mary shook her head as if she understood,
but I had the feeling that what Sam told us
confused her.

We waited for Father and when we walked
home, I asked, "Why do the people of
Weymouth keep gunpowder and rifles in the
meetinghouse?"

"Because, Nabby, the meetinghouse is the
safest place," Father explained. "It's dry up
in the garret, and there aren't any fireplaces
and chimneys from which sparks can fly and
set the gunpowder afire."

"What if it stormed and lightning hit the
steeple?" Mary asked nervously.

"That would start a fire," Father said.

"Why do we have to have gunpowder and
guns?" I asked.

"All towns must be prepared," Father
explained. "Towns north of us need ammuni-
tion to fight the French and Indians. We
don't need it for those purposes because your
Grandfather Quincy made friends with the
Indians in our part of the country. You should
be aware of that, Nabby, after knowing what
a friendly part the Indians played in your
christening."

"Then why do we have gunpowder and
guns?" I asked.

"We are safe as long as we have the
English Navy to protect us," Father said.
"But we take precautions in case the Navy
couldn't help us when a need came."

By this time we had come to the blacksmith's shop and Father went inside to talk to

the men and learn the news from Boston.

It was then I missed Will. "Have you seen Will, Mary?" I asked my sister.

"I hope he hasn't run off again!" Mary exclaimed. "Mother expects us to watch out for him, you know."

We called, "Will!" There was no answer. "Will!"

We looked up and down Church Street.

Finally we saw him in an open field in back of the blacksmith's. He was with three older boys who had muskets. When we got close to them I heard Will say, "The key's up over the doorway to the garret."

"Will!" I shouted at him, "You are not supposed to tell that!"

"That's all right," the big boy, Isaac grinned. "We just want a little gunpowder for our muskets."

"That gunpowder is there for grown-ups' guns in case we need to fight an enemy," I told him.

"The French and Indians don't come around here and besides we've got the English Navy to protect us," Ebin said.

"Nobody will know the difference anyway. Nobody will see us. We'll be as quiet as ghosts," Benjamin added.

"Ghosts aren't quiet," I told them. "Phoebe says they make an awful scary noise."

"You won't tell I told about the gunpowder, will you, Nabby?" Will asked. "You won't tell, will you?" His voice sounded smothered with fear. "Promise, Nabby, promise," he begged. "Father would be in a fury if he knew! Promise!"

I didn't want to promise, but Will was in such a state. And Father was just coming from the blacksmith's—I blurted out the words, "I promise."

And the moment I said it I was sorry I had promised.

I was unhappy. What would God think about what I had done? I knew I had to stop the boys from taking any gunpowder. I knew that even being near gunpowder was dangerous. Besides, if they took a little this time, what would stop them from taking even more the next time? Gradually they could take so much that the supply wouldn't be enough to help the townspeople if they were attacked. Most of all, I was helping boys to steal, and there was no doubt that that was wrong.

I knew I should tell Father. Still, Father always said a promise is a sacred trust. It must not be broken. What was I to do?

I went to bed early and Mother was glad I was taking extra rest. She was always worrying about my health. But I wasn't thinking about my health on this night. I was thinking about the boys and how they could blow up the whole town or, at the very least, rob the town of its only defense. What was I to do?

I sat at my bedroom window and looked out into the peaceful night. I prayed and asked God to show me the right answer. I could hear the clock tick. I could hear Rover, our dog, yawning as he lay by the fireplace downstairs.

Listening to Rover gave me a thought. He barked when it was important to bark. He was a good dog, always aware of what was going on around him. If Rover was at the meetinghouse when the boys came there, he would bark. His bark would awaken the sexton. The sexton would chase the boys away and everything would be all right.

Rover was the answer to my prayers! I would take Rover to the meetinghouse. Quickly I dressed, threw on a warm shawl, and crept down the stairs. Rover came into the entry way. I patted him and whispered in his ear to follow me. We ran all the way to the meetinghouse. I was hoping we were in time.

We were. When we got inside the building we heard footsteps. I told Rover to be quiet and pulled him with me up the steps to the balcony.

I ran to the garret door and tried the knob. It opened! Father must have forgotten to lock the door. I pushed Rover in, closed the door, and sat down beside him on the bottom step.

Immediately after that I heard the boys' voices.

One said, "Did you hear something?"

Another said, "Yes. It sounded like something dragging across a floor."

The third boy said, "If it is a ghost, we'll fight him together." His voice shook and trembled.

Rover scratched at the garret door. He wanted to get out.

A boy's voice said, "I think I heard a hoof. An old lady told me once that the devil has hoofs. And I'm going home this very minute."

"You stay right here," the first boy's voice said. "I'll go first. Come on. Follow me."

When the footsteps sounded on the top step, I thought Rover would bark, but he didn't. He nuzzled closer to me. I had to do something quickly. Suddenly I thought about the boys' fear of ghosts and I let out a most mournful ghost-like moan. It was such a loud moan that it bounced on the walls of the meetinghouse and echoed back.

Then there was the noise of running and scrambling on the stairs. The sounds of the boys' running feet came up to the garret, and I knew they were racing for their homes.

Rover and I went home. He hadn't barked to awaken the sexton as I had planned, but we had saved the gunpowder all the same. At the entry way Rover left me to return to the fireside, and I returned to my bed. Dreamily I hoped I wouldn't have to be a ghost again as I fell asleep smiling.

It was another clear night, many weeks later, when I had almost forgotten about the boys trying to take gunpowder from the meetinghouse, that I was awakened by a bright light in my room. I knew it couldn't be the sun. I turned toward Mary, who shared my bed, and tried to wake her.

"Mary, Mary," I said. "Wake up. Our room is light and it isn't morning yet."

Mary blinked. "The light is so bright! It's flickering," she stammered.

I heard loud crackling noises outside and then Father came running up the stairs calling, "Abigail! Mary! Wake up! The meetinghouse is on fire! Our home may be next!" Father dashed into our room and pulled the coverlets from our bed.

"Father!" Mary cried, "What are you doing with our covers?"

"There is no time to dress, Mary," Father's deep voice was vibrant with excitement. "Wrap yourselves in the coverlets and put on your shoes."

"What about the others?" I gasped as I tugged with the shoe ribbons.

"Your mother has Baby Betsey and Will was the first to see the fire. He woke us."

Mary was screaming and holding on to the bedpost. She was helpless with fear. I knew I had to help Mary with her shoes. She couldn't seem to move.

Father saw what was happening and he forced Mary's shoe on one foot and then handed me the other foot and the shoe.

Mother's voice came up to us from below. She was calling Father and telling him that the flames at the meetinghouse were climbing to the steeple.

"Abigail," Father shouted, "the town's gunpowder is stored in the steeple. It may blow up any minute. Run!"

Father pushed me ahead of him down the steep steps. I almost lost my balance. I swayed dizzily. I heard Mary moan. She was so limp Father gathered her up in his arms and carried her down the stairs.

When we got outside the parsonage, I saw a long line of men passing leather water buckets from the well to the parsonage where they threw the water on the house.

"We'll save your house, Reverend," one of the men said. "We're dampening it down good. But we can't save the meetinghouse."

"There's gunpowder in the meetinghouse," Father shouted. "It may blow up any minute. Run! Save yourselves!"

Instantly everyone began to push and shove. I saw people running in every direction, their eyes wild with fear. I saw Will helping Mother who was carrying Baby Betsey close in her arms. I grabbed on to Father's cloak and we ran. Father was still carrying Mary in his arms.

Then there was a thunderous noise. The dark sky above turned red. Flaming boards flew through the air like birds of fire. I fell over something and then everything went quiet and black.

When I opened my eyes I was lying on the gound. Father was sitting beside me and had thrown his cloak over me. The air hung with smoke and was hard to breath.

"What's happened?" I asked.

"The men saved the parsonage with their water buckets," Father said.

I saw Mother sitting on the ground not far away. She was cradling Mary in her arms. Mary buried her face in Mother's shoulder. A sob escaped her lips now and then.

Mother said, "Come girls, we must make a good breakfast for all our friends."

I took Mary's hand and we walked back to the house together. Some of the men who had worked in the bucket brigade walked with us.

As they walked along they talked about the fire. I heard many men ask each other, "How do you suppose the fire started?"

No one seemed to know. Father said, "A small spark could have been the cause. It has been dry, you know, and a single spark, like a spark from a foot warmer, could have started a fire."

A foot warmer — a foot warmer. I began remembering what I had seen at Sunday services.

I remembered the Simpsons were the last to come to services. Mr. Simpson, one of the richest sheepmen in Massachusetts, explained that he had been shearing sheep until long after the sun had gone down the night

before and had overslept this Sabbath morning. Mrs. Simpson had explained to Father
that she had been feeling poorly these last
few days and was grateful that she could
come at all.

"But for the foot warmer," she said, "I
would be obliged to stay home."

It was then that I noticed Mr. Simpson was
carrying a square iron box filled with hot
coals for the comfort of Mrs. Simpson's feet.

As soon as Father began his sermon I saw
Mr. Simpson slump down in his seat, and I
knew that Mr. Trowbridge, the tithing man,
saw Mr. Simpson too. Mr. Trowbridge
carried the long stick in his hand as he did at
every church service. The stick had a brass
knob on one end. Mr. Trowbridge walked
about the church during services to make
sure no one went to sleep. I saw him come
toward Mr. Simpson. Suddenly there was a
loud "wham" as the brass knob was brought
down on Mr. Simpson's head.

Blinking his eyes, Mr. Simpson jumped to
his feet. He shouted, "Stand still!" Then,
grabbing his wife by her shoulders, he began
to shake her.

"Wake up, Henry!" Mrs. Simpson shouted
at him. "I'm not one of your sheep. I'm your
wife. You're not shearing sheep, you're
listening to Reverend Smith's sermon."

There were giggles all around. All eyes
were on the Simpsons. Even Father stopped
speaking for the moment. I wanted to giggle
too, but I knew the pastor's daughter should
not show merriment at such an awkward
time.

Mrs. Simpson was blushing a strawberry
red. She took little Hannah's hand and

pushed her husband out of the pew. I remember hearing something clatter when Mrs. Simpson left the pew.

A little later, when I was back home, I happened to look out the window, and I saw Mr. Simpson ride up to the meetinghouse in his wagon. I thought maybe he was looking for the tithing man and that maybe he was going to hit him because the tithing man had given him such a big whack. But I decided that that wasn't why Mr. Simpson had come back to the meetinghouse. He wouldn't fight with Mr. Trowbridge on the Lord's day.

At dinner, as soon as prayers were said, I told Father about Mr. Simpson. "Hannah Simpson said the reason Mr. Trowbridge hit her father so hard was because Mr. Simpson caught him cheating on wool weight when he sold his wool to Mr. Trowbridge."

Father looked at me. He was serious. He said, "You should speak no evil of anyone, Abigail. Even if you know evil to be true, you should not repeat it."

I felt ashamed. Father had told me before not to gossip. I said no more. Then Mother and Father talked of a new meetinghouse which was to be built at once, everyone in the congregation contributing his share of goods and services.

But I wondered, during the next few days, what Mr. Simpson had been doing at the meetinghouse after services.

On the day when the whole town gathered to start building the new meetinghouse, Paul Torrey, the schoolmaster, told Father, "I believe I know who started the fire."

"Do you have proof?" Father asked. "Did you see anyone go near the meetinghouse after services?"

I looked at Mr. Simpson who was standing nearby. I wondered if he would admit he had been back after services.

Mr. Simpson stepped forward. "I went back, Reverend Smith," he said. "I went back for our foot warmer."

"That's correct, Reverend," the tithing man stepped forward too. "Mr. Simpson came to my house later for his foot warmer. I picked it up for him after the service. I knew it was my fault that he left in such a hurry and forgot the warmer."

"How did you know Mr. Trowbridge had your foot warmer?" Father asked, turning his full gaze on Mr. Simpson.

Mr. Simpson hurried to explain. "I didn't think about the foot warmer when I went to Mr. Trowbridge's house. I decided to go there because we had had a misunderstanding about my wool. I found out that I was wrong and he was right. I wanted to tell him so."

Father turned his eyes on me when he said, "It is good to have two such righteous men in our congregation."

I blushed. I knew Father was telling me that this was an example of what he'd been talking about—never repeat evil.

Still I remembered the sound of something making a noise on the floor when Mrs. Simpson pushed Mr. Simpson out of the pew.

After lessons, the next morning, I told Father that I still wasn't sure that the noise I had heard wasn't the warmer being turned over.

"No one is sure," nodded Father. In a thoughtful vein he continued, "Mr. Simpson might not have noticed coals smoldering when he came back after the service. He is a devout and kindly man. He would be deeply grieved if he thought he could have set fire to the meetinghouse."

We had a long silence as we pondered together.

Then Father said, "However, I must write an account of the fire in the record book, and I shall." Father wrote:

Weymouth Meetinghouse took fire April 23, 1751. Burned to the ground in 2 hours. 3 bbls of gunpowder, the town stock, blew up with great noise. Uncertain how it happened.

As Father closed the record book I thought the incident of the meetinghouse fire was shut away. But in a few years it was to be thought about again at a most unusual time and place.

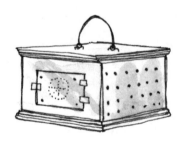

Chapter III

At Grandmother Quincy's

I knew my life was going to change after hearing Mother and Father talking. I was at the window at the far end of our wide, sweet-smelling kitchen slicing apples for pies. Mother and Father were alone at the table which was unusual. At the parsonage there was always someone around who had dropped in. Many came from long distances with their families and had to be fed and put up for the night. Mother and Father were always busy taking care of people's needs in our home. It was one of the ways they had of doing God's work.

My parents were a living example of a Bible verse I had heard: "Be ye kind one to another, tenderhearted, forgiving one another, even as God for Christ's sake hath forgiven you" (Ephesians 4:32).

"All our extra visitors have made a lot of work," Father said, settling himself at the kitchen table.

"Phoebe and I couldn't begin to do all the work ourselves," Mother said. "We've put too much on Abigail."

I wanted to interrupt and say that I didn't mind. In fact I liked all the comings and goings of people who brought news of what was going on outside of Weymouth.

"Abigail has never complained," Mother was quick to add. "She's helped with the cooking and dishwashing and baking, most willingly."

"And serving food and looking after the

smaller children," Father added. "But there hasn't even been enough time for Nabby's lessons." Father looked worried.

"And certainly no time for talk about manners," Mother nodded. She too looked worried. "Abigail's getting too thin. Her health has never been good. She's had colds every winter and an occasional bout of rheumatism too."

It was customary to talk about my health. I was slightly built and only five foot and two inches tall. I looked smaller than that when standing near Mother or Mary. They were large women with heavy set shoulders and thick forearms. Even my younger brother Billy was already taller than me.

I looked out the window where Billy's colt was kicking up his heels in the pasture, and thought, "Size has nothing to do with strength. Billy's colt looks delicate, still he's strong like me. I can race all the way up Burying Hill and back and not be out of breath."

Father was up on his feet pacing the kitchen thoughtfully. Then he said: "There is reason to be concerned about Nabby. I didn't want to tell you but there is a health problem here in Weymouth."

"What health problem?" I blurted out before Mother did.

"A terrible throat disease has broken out," Father said. "It is a strange malady. It doesn't seem to come to grown people, but children get the disease. Some are dying of it."

"Oh!" cried Mother. It was easy to see she was startled by the news the way her eyes widened and her voice quivered.

"Ben has it," Father said. "The Simpsons's daughter has it, too."

"Then Abigail is sure to take it," Mother cried. "With the history of consumption in the Quincy family . . ."

"It's best we send Nabby to your mother's," Father decided. "Tom will take her in the morning."

At that minute I finished peeling apples and began to think about packing. Just think, Grandmother Quincy's!

Remembering the sea chest in the attic, I decided to fill it with presents for Grandmother. "Mary, Mary!" I called, running up the stairs. "Help me get the sea chest!"

"Why, Nabby? What do you want the chest for?" Mary ran out of her room and followed close behind me.

"I'm going to Braintree to visit Grandmother Quincy!"

We finally got the chest in our room and I ran out to the barn and got a sack of straw and one of bran and a bag of cracked corn.

Mother followed me upstairs and when she saw the three sacks on the bed, she doubled up with laughter.

"Why are my presents for Grandmother funny?" I asked.

"Because, dear Nabby, Grandmother has no need of these. She has all the grain she needs in her big barn. You don't have to take presents," Mother explained.

"You always take presents when you go for a visit," I said feeling a little hurt and confused. "When you go to Boston to visit Aunt Elizabeth, you take boxes and boxes of things."

"Aunt Elizabeth lives in a town. She doesn't have farm foods, so I take her sausage, butter, and other produce that is hard for her to get fresh in Boston."

Mary cut in. "Mother gets pins, spices, dyes, and fabrics from Aunt Elizabeth. Remember? Things we don't have in the country."

But Mother let me take the sea chest and Mary helped me pile my petticoats and Sunday dresses into it. I packed my new shoes and a bonnet and shawl along with my nightgowns.

"I still want to take Grandmother a present," I told Mary as we packed.

"Take her the sampler you just finished, Nabby," Mary suggested.

"It's a lovely sampler," Mother smiled. "There is not one misplaced or poorly worked stitch in it."

I wasn't sure it was nice enough for

Grandmother Quincy's mansion, but since
Mary and Mother thought it was so nice it
was placed on top of my things in the chest.

That night, before cuddling between the
homespun flannel sheets that Mother and I
had woven, I prayed to the Lord to help me
please Grandmother and that my visit to
Braintree would be a happy one. I thought,
"And all things whatsoever ye shall ask in
prayer, believing, ye shall receive" (Matthew
21:22). I lapsed into sweet sleep and dreamed
of all the boys and girls I would meet at
Braintree and the parties I would go to, and
the trips to Boston I would take. But most of
all I dreamed about Grandfather Quincy's
library with all his books to read. In my
dreams I saw Grandmother—her smile, her
soft laugh, her elegant manners.

It was the rattle of the cart and Tom's
talking to the team below my window that
wakened me the next morning.

Mother called, "Nabby! Tom's ready with
the team hitched and the sea chest strapped
on. Quickly child! Breakfast is ready."

I threw back the covers and wriggled into
my clothes. This was the day to make my trip
to Mount Wollaston!

Soon it was time. Father lifted me up to
the seat. He called to the horses and down
the hill we went.

A salty breeze almost pushed the words
back into my mouth as I called good-byes to
all the neighbors. I saw Ben at his window
and waved. "Please get well!" I called. He
nodded, but I knew he couldn't hear me.

"You ought to be more careful, Miss," Tom
said.

It was then I realized that the way I was

jumping up and down and waving wildly and
calling out good-byes wasn't being ladylike.
Mother would most certainly disapprove. I
sat down. From then on I bowed and nodded
very nicely to all my other friends who were
waving their good-byes.

It was a lovely day, a salty day, a God's
blessing day. The road was dry. Knowing
every twist and curve in it, I knew we'd turn
and come out along the seashore. Soon I
heard the gentle waves, their lips kissing the
shore. I saw a flick of a red-winged bird and
heard the gulls' harsh calls.

The four miles to Grandmother's rolled by
and soon we came to the Quincy's acres. I
waved to the men working in Grandfather's
stone quarry.

Several of the men called out: "Welcome to
Mount Wollaston, Miss Nabby!"

Towering above us was Grandmother's
house on the hill, and Tom pulled at the reins
as we turned into the lane. It was the first
time I had ever come here alone and I felt
grown-up and important.

Grandfather and Grandmother were waiting for me on the front steps. As soon as the
cart stopped Grandfather lifted me down and
Grandmother opened her arms to me. I
hugged and kissed her.

Then Grandfather said, "See here, young
lady, I have a kiss or two for you too."

"There is a present for you, Grandmother," I said as soon as we were in the entry
way. "There were lots of things to bring you,
but Mother said you didn't need them."

Lifting the chest's lid, I took out the
sampler.

Grandmother's eyes widened and a pretty

smile curved her lips. "I am pleased,
Abigail," she said. "The sampler is beautifully done, dear. And what's important is
that you wanted to give something of
yourself; something in which you gave effort
and time. This I appreciate."

Grandmother put the sampler on the
candle table in the entry way where everyone would see it.

Closing the lid on the chest, we followed
Tom as he carried it up the stairs.

Grandmother sat near the window of the
cheerful room that was to be mine during my
visit at Wollaston, as I continued to unpack.
Being busy made it easier to tell Grandmother what really worried me.

"It's going to be hard to remember not to
run or skip or jump," I said. "And I don't like
being out of things."

"What things?" Grandmother asked.

"I don't like not knowing what's going on in
the world until the men tell me. I didn't even
know when Governor Shirley of our colony
was recalled to England last September. But
Mother says it's not important to know."

"Women do not take as active a part in the
outside world as men," Grandmother told
me. "But women do Christian deeds that are
as great as the deeds men do. You will see
how much good you can do in the world if you
watch and listen to what goes on about you."

After I unpacked I ran out to play on the
wide, green lawns that sloped down to the
sea. The salt air made me want to breathe
deeply. It was as if God was filling me with
strength.

The next morning at breakfast I asked
Grandmother when we would be meeting

some of the boys and girls of Braintree. I was anxious to meet new people, especially those who knew what was happening in the world.

"When you learn to be a fine hostess," Abigail," Grandmother said, "we shall entertain."

That afternoon the maid set out the best tea things. Grandmother was dressed in one of her heavy silk dresses and wore a cap made of lace from across the sea. Grandmother poured tea into four cups even though just the two of us sat there. She asked me to pass the cups around and then the cakes. I curtsied at each empty chair. I thought it was quite an elegant pretend party.

Grandmother smiled when I was through practicing and said, "You did everything properly, Abby. Now you must keep practicing even when you go back home."

"It won't be like this, Grandmother," I said. "We don't have china as fine as yours. We don't have a silver teapot."

"The serving things are not as important as the *way* you serve," Grandmother said. "If you keep Godly thoughts and pleasant manners, you could serve from a simple clay pot and still have a party. And now I shall invite some guests."

Friends and relatives had noticed I was a young lady now, and my little-girl "Nabby" was gradually giving way to a grown-up sounding "Abby."

It was two days before the guests would arrive. Since Grandmother had many servants there was no work for me to do. I spent most of my time curled up in the big leather chair in the library reading books.

Then party day came. "Grandmother, what shall I do when I am presented?"

"You must curtsy naturally, and offer the gentlemen your hand. Above all, dear, speak softly for that is the first requirement of a lady," Grandmother said.

"Who will be coming?" I asked.

Grandmother studied the list lying on her writing desk. "A gentleman who was one time a neighbor, John Hancock. I've invited your cousin, Dorothy Quincy. Joseph Warren will be coming. Then there is John Adams who is home for the summer holidays. He teaches at Worchester. He was at Harvard with the other boys."

"Doesn't John Adams live in Braintree?" I asked, suddenly remembering that Father had spoken about him.

"The Adams farm is about a mile from here," Grandmother nodded.

"Is he going to be a minister?" I asked, thinking it was an intelligent question. Almost every New England family, who had the money for higher education, expected their oldest son to be a minister.

Grandmother shook her head sadly. "No, I fear not," she said. "John Adams is foolishly studying law. He'll not amount to much that way, earning his fees by helping the dishonest. People in the colonies don't think much of lawyers."

I wanted to disagree with Grandmother and point out to her that sometimes people are falsely accused and need a lawyer, but she was already laying out the tea things.

The silver tea service gleamed on a small table and Grandmother measured the tea and put a copper kettle on the fire.

"When the guests are here, you may pass the plate of teacakes, Nabby, as I pour the tea," Grandmother instructed.

I watched Grandmother making ready for the company. She moved easily among the appointments of the drawing room. The rich silk of her full-skirted dress shimmered as she walked.

In a few minutes there was the sound of horses' hoofs and soon I was curtsying beside Grandmother and greeting our guests.

My cousin, Dorothy wasn't much older than me, but she knew more about being in male company. She had already had a proposal of marriage! She looked at the men with her dark eyes coyly and yet intensely.

The three men were more interesting to me than Dorothy. John Hancock, who lived in Boston, was thin and stooped and slightly nervous. His wig was elegant and was tied with a big, black bow. His red velvet coat had large engraved buttons.

Joseph Warren was still going to Harvard. He planned to be a doctor of medicine.

But the man who interested me most was John Adams. He was the oldest of the three. He had beautiful blue eyes. He didn't wear a wig, but wore his light-brown hair neatly combed. He was short and stocky with shoulders that were broad and powerful. He talked more than the others with a deep voice. When he laughed, he laughed heartily.

Just as one of John Adams' laughs died away Grandfather Quincy strode into the room. He was smiling.

"It is good news, sir?" asked John Hancock.

Since Grandfather was interested in government and a colonel in the local militia, the young men looked to him for government news.

"Our new prime minister in England, William Pitt, has sent us Lord Jeffrey Amherst. His ships are in Boston Harbor now."

The English, I knew, wanted to move westward and take farm land on the other side of the mountains. But the French claimed the Mississippi Valley as well as land

in Canada. The Indians were on the side of
the French because they wanted this land for
hunting. Father had said that the French and
English had been fighting for more than fifty
years.

Grandfather went on, "Wolfe is to move
against Quebec, and Amherst is to go by way
of Lake Champlain to Montreal, and then join
Wolfe."

"It will be good for the English to win,"
said John Adams. "When this war is over we
will not need England's protection any
longer."

"How disloyal!" I thought.

"Why should we want to break away from
England?" asked Grandfather. "We have the
rights of all English-born people and we have
been prosperous and well cared for under
English rule."

"Her navigation laws hurt our trade," said
John Adams.

I thought, "He is a very persistent person.
He thinks his ideas are right. Grandfather
likes him even if he doesn't agree with him. I
can see that. I like him too."

After the guests left, Grandfather said,
"That John Adams is an unusual man."

"In what way?" Grandmother asked.

"Well, for example, as Adams left I
suggested that we talked too much politics
and that perhaps he would have been more
interested in talking to the girls. You know
what he said?"

"I'm sure we have no idea," Grandmother
said.

"He said he expects to go to Boston soon
to practice law and that means he will have to
give all of his time to law. He said there was

no room in his life for girls, guns or cards," Grandfather said.

Then Grandfather went on, "Adams told me that he wants a thinking woman, a reading woman. He said those are very scarce in New England."

I smiled at that. Most girls never went beyond the Dame's School. It was not fashionable to be educated. Perhaps I was the only girl in New England whose parents and grandparents had encouraged to do a great deal of reading.

Grandfather's voice came through my private thinking. He was saying: "Abby, don't you hear me? I asked you if you would like to accompany me to Boston tomorrow. You could visit some of the Smith relatives while I watch Lord Jeffrey Amherst land."

"Oh, yes, Grandfather," I said in a voice I knew was too loud to please Grandmother. I was so excited my voice got loud before I realized it.

But Grandmother said nothing. She did raise a reproving finger though. Then she said, "We shall get you ready. You must rise at dawn, Abby."

"Yes, Grandmother!" I cried and skipped from the room.

Chapter IV

Boisterous Boston

The sun was up when Grandfather Quincy
and I arrived at Boston. The wheels rattled
over the cobblestone streets, and I watched
country people in their wagons coming to
Boston to sell their berries and squash.

"Look at all the ships!" I cried, pointing
toward the bay. "I've never seen so many
ships at once!"

"Lord Amherst's ships are idling in the
harbor. There is a whaling fleet in too, and
your Uncle Isaac's ship is in," Grandfather
explained.

Suddenly the coach stopped. It swayed
crazily at the suddenness of the halt. As I
looked out the coach window, I gasped. Two

sailors with rings in their ears and knives in their belts, stood blocking the road.

"Are they pirates, Grandfather?"

"No, Abby," he said. "These men are sailors who have taken on some heathen ways."

"What is the meaning of this?" Grandfather shouted to the men. "Take your hands off my horses. I demand you to step aside!"

I was proud of my Grandfather. My fear slipped away. His strong voice and his commanding attitude and his tall, vigorous body gave me strength.

"Oh, it is you, Colonel Quincy," said the taller man politely. "We're from Isaac Smith's ship with orders from Mr. Smith not to let anyone loiter around the docks. They're unloading now, you see, sir. The cargo is a very expensive one. Mostly dyes, sir. Dyes are worth almost as much as gold, sir."

"Yes, yes," said Grandfather with an impatient wave of his hand. We rattled on.

"We'll get off at the end of Long Wharf," Grandfather told the driver, Job. "You may wait for me at The Crown."

Long Wharf was two thousand feet long, stretching into the sea. It was the longest wharf in Boston. Ships of all kinds were anchored on the south side. There were whalers, merchant vessels, small fishing boats, and ships of the king's navy. On the north side of the wharf were warehouses, shops, and counting houses.

I sniffed the air. It smelled different from the air at Weymouth. At Weymouth a breeze smelled of clover and rich earth. Here the smells came from dried fish, leather, lumber, salted meats. Over all the heavy odor of molasses hung with a sweet stickiness.

Grandfather explained that the molasses had come from the West Indies. It would be made into rum in the colonies. Then the rum would be exchanged for slaves.

After our long, windy walk, we came to the place where Uncle Isaac Smith's ship was docked. The crew was working as fast as they could, hoisting goods from the hold of the ship. Some sailors were loading wheelbarrows and moving them down the gangplank and up the street to the warehouse. They were having a hard time pushing the wheelbarrows for the streets were crowded now, and the sailors had to maneuver the wheelbarrows between the people. The townspeople had come to see the troops land.

I was pushed and shoved. I wondered how I'd ever get to see the landing. Then a tall man came out of one of the warehouses and after bowing slightly, said, "Colonel Quincy, I'd be honored if you and your charming granddaughter would come to the second story of my warehouse. You can view the landing of His Gracious Majesty's troops from there."

Grandfather nodded and bid me follow him. He walked with such big steps that I had to take two or three steps to his one. I followed Grandfather to the warehouse and up the narrow steps to the second floor. I was relieved that I was going to be able to see the landing.

Leaning out the window I could see Boston Harbor and all the patchwork of roofs which ran to the water's edge. Outlined against the blue sky were the tall hills of Boston. There was Fort Hill on the south, Beacon Hill in the middle, and Copp's Hill on the north.

Then the bells began to ring so loudly I covered my ears.

Grandfather pulled my hands down ever so gently as he said, "Abby, I want you to hear the drums and the whistle of the fifes. This is a proud day for us Englishmen."

I did listen and look. Lines of uniformed men with their long-tailed red coats and their white breeches, passed by the warehouse. The officers rode well-groomed horses.

At the end of the marching men was Lord Jeffrey Amherst, riding on a large bay. As he passed the warehouse he took off his plumed hat and doffed it toward the cheering crowd.

A cheer came to my throat too and I shouted, "Hurrah! Hurrah!" I was proud to be English. I thought it was grand to have these trained troops defend the colonies against the French and Indians. I thought for a fleeting moment about John Adams and how ungrateful he was toward the mother country.

"It's wonderful to be English," I told Grandfather. In my mind I was talking to John Adams.

"Yes, indeed," agreed Grandfather. "But we cannot linger here any longer. Uncle Isaac and Aunt Elizabeth will be expecting you. We must be on our way."

Uncle Isaac and Aunt Elizabeth's house was almost as elegant as Grandmother's. It was on top of Copp's Hill and from the generous windows I could see ten or more shipyards. I could hear the sound of hammers and saws. The smell of paint wafted up from the yards. Boston was an exciting place!

My room was wide and pleasant. Aunt Elizabeth sent servants to open my bed. They brought me fresh milk to drink. They arranged flowers in my room and laid out the clothes I was to wear.

"Aunt Elizabeth, I would be spoiled if I stayed here in Boston for a very long time."

"Nonsense child," she stroked my hair with her jeweled hand. "You've always been a delicate child, Abby. You could do with a little spoiling. Despite your frequent illnesses, you've grown to be a very pretty young lady. The young men in Boston will be coming to call."

Her remark made me think about John Adams and then I felt a blush warm my cheeks. But Aunt Elizabeth hadn't noticed. She was busy hanging up clothes and smoothing the sheets of the huge four-poster bed.

The next morning Grandfather woke me even before the venders on the street began calling out their wares.

"We have a big day ahead, child," he said. "We must stop at Paul Revere's for a teapot he is making for your Grandmother, and I do want to take this opportunity to go aboard Isaac's ship."

Job, Grandfather's driver, was ready at the door and we drove through the steep North End street until we came near the head of Clark's Wharf. We stopped in front of a dark brown house with small-paned windows.

The smell of charcoal was strong in the shop. The man sitting at the bench, looked up and smiled as he said, "Good morning, Colonel Quincy. And this young lady with you looks like a Quincy too. Am I correct in addressing her as Miss Quincy?"

"May I present my granddaughter, Abigail Smith?" Grandfather said and I felt he was proud to introduce me.

I curtsied as Grandmother had taught me and looked into Paul Revere's dark eyes. He had dark skin and a wide mouth. He wasn't a tall man, but he was a sturdy man. I remembered Grandmother had said he was of French decent and that his ancestors had come to America to escape religious persecution much as our ancestors had come from England for the same reason.

"Do you have my wife's silver piece ready?" Grandfather asked.

"Yes, sir," said Paul Revere. "I finished it quickly for I knew you'd be here today because of Lord Amherst's arrival. I believe with you, sir, that Amherst and Wolfe will conquer the French and that will be the end of this long and tedious conflict."

A fish peddler went by, at that moment, blowing his tin horn, and I didn't hear what further political opinion Grandfather gave.

Grandfather paid Mr. Revere for the teapot and we went back to the carriage. Job drove us to Uncle Isaac's warehouse. Since Uncle Isaac was a wealthy merchant, he had the time and leisure to spend with Grandfather and me.

At Uncle Isaac's warehouse there was a mixture of smells that my nose had never sniffed before. They tingled my imagination. Their aromas spoke to me of faraway places. There was the smell of nutmegs and ginger. I could smell coffee too. We walked through sawdust, spilled on the floor as fine porcelains and china dishes were unpacked from wooden boxes. The workmen called the sawdust "bran" and things that were shipped in this bran were called "bran new."

"And now," said Uncle Isaac, "would you like to visit one of my ships?"

"Oh, yes!" I told him, looking up into his kindly face. "I've never been on board a ship before."

We walked under the elms toward the wharf. I paused and waited for a gold thrush to break the calm. His notes swelled into a triumphant psalm. The men paid little attention to my skipping and hopping as I followed them. It wasn't ladylike, but I was so excited about boarding a ship that I couldn't stand still.

Grandfather was saying, "Once Quebec falls, all our strife will be over. All of Canada will belong to England."

"Long live the King!" said Uncle Isaac.

At the wharf a sailor helped us into a rowboat and rowed us to one of the ships anchored in the harbor.

When we came to the ship the sailor helped me put my foot on the first rung of a rope ladder that was hanging over the side of the ship. I was afraid. The ladder swayed in the breeze and didn't look strong enough to support even my small weight. But Uncle Isaac and Grandfather nodded for me to climb. Taking a deep breath, I did. It was easy, once I got started.

On board the captain greeted us warmly. "Let me take you to my quarters," he said.

His cabin was small with a bunk on one side and a great table on the other. The table was covered with maps, charts, quills, ink, and small tools.

Then, back on deck, we watched some of the sailors climb the ship's rigging. Sailors were swabbing decks, others were pushing barrels of cargo. They yelled to each other and evil words sputtered from their mouths like sparks from a roaring fire.

"Grandfather," I whispered. Grandfather bent down to hear me better. "Grandfather," I said, "these are foul men!"

"No, dear," Grandfather whispered back. "Many of them have not had the opportunity to hear the Lord's Word. They do not know the words they use are sinful."

"How sad!" I cried. "I shall pray for them, Grandfather."

"As shall I," he said.

The ship was rocking ever so slightly. The rocking bothered me. My stomach began churning. I felt dizzy too.

"Please, may we go back to shore now?" I asked.

Uncle Isaac patted my head sympathetically. "Now, now, Abby," he said, "don't let a little uneasiness make you want to abandon the sea. Someday you will take a long voyage across the ocean. So, you must accept and enjoy the rolling of the sea."

"I don't think I ever will," I said as the churning in my stomach grew worse.

Of course, on this day, I had no way of knowing that Uncle Isaac's prediction that I would someday take an ocean voyage would indeed come true.

The swooping sea gulls shrieked above us as we were rowed to shore. It was with gratefulness that I felt solid land under my feet once more.

The weathered face of Boston bid us welcome.

This visit at Grandmother Quincy's was over, but I knew there would be many more exciting ones.

Chapter V

John Adams

As the next four years went by, I made many trips to Boston and to Grandmother Quincy's. Grandmother and I were kindred souls. Grandmother too had taken Christ as her Savior. She loved God and admired common sense. She liked to laugh also.

One day when I was at Grandmother's, Mrs. Tittle of whom Grandmother was not especially fond, came for tea. I assisted with serving as usual. The maid handed me a tray of freshly baked cherry tarts. They smelled deliciously of butter and cherries and almonds.

Mrs. Tittle was talking rapidly and vehemently about being loyal to the crown. She

waved her hands expressively. Even the long
elegant feather which was attached to her
imported lace cap, waved about as she
nodded and jerked her head to emphasize the
points of loyalty she was making.

I was so fascinated by Mrs. Tittle's
movements I neglected to watch my tarts.
When I did glance at the tarts I gasped
silently at what I saw. Mrs. Tittle's feather
was dragging back and forth, back and forth
across the tarts, absorbing the red, bubbling
cherry juices!

Grandmother appeared not to notice. She
gave her full attention to the very verbal
Mrs. Tittle.

When at last I escorted Mrs. Tittle to the
door, I hurried back into Grandmother's
sitting room to apologize.

Something in the twinkling lights in
Grandmother's eyes made me pause to study
her pretty face.

Then Grandmother said, "Now Mrs. Tittle
not only has a tart tongue, but she has a tart
feather as well."

I could no longer hold back the laughter.
Grandmother threw back her head and her
deep-throated laugh joined mine. In fact we
laughed to such an extent that Grandfather
Quincy left his study to investigate the cause
of such merriment.

There were other pleasures at Grandmother's too. We read and talked about the
Bible together.

The large collection of books at Wollaston
were all mine to enjoy. I read the histories of
England and prayed every night for the king
and the royal family. I read the works of
Shakespeare and Pope. Grandmother gave

me British periodicals. *The Spectator* contained witty essays written in a fine style which we read and talked about together. I made these my literary model. There were many books on religion which influenced my writing and thinking too.

Grandmother and Grandfather's house was always filled with boys and girls from the neighborhood who came on horseback or in horse-drawn sulkies, chaises or, in winter, sleighs. We always had fun at Wollaston playing games or having long discussions of poetry, history, literature, art, and Jesus' ministry.

If weather or sickness kept us home there was always the chance to communicate by letters. Many of my friends signed their letters with pen names taken from mythology or from the classics. I always signed my letters "Diana."

There was a constant exchange of letters with boys and girls, but never with a sweetheart. Many of my friends were getting married. But few men called on me. Mary said it was because men were afraid of a girl who was so much better educated than they were. Mary knew about these things. She was engaged to Richard Cranch.

One evening early in October, while Mary was waiting for Richard, I murmured my thoughts out loud to her. "I'm seventeen. Old enough to be married."

Smoothing my hands over the old brown calico which I had made myself, and stroking my hair which was swept back like two wings on either side of my face, I waited for Mary's consoling words.

"You're so lovely, Abby," Mary said. "You

move with grace and dignity. Grandmother
Quincy should be proud of how well her
teaching has taken effect."

Just then there was a knock. "It's
Richard!" cried Mary. She was still arranging
her hair before the mirror. "Please let
Richard in."

I wasn't looking neat enough to receive
visitors, but Mary was so excited and happy I
couldn't deny her request. Mary was in love
with Richard Cranch who was an English
born gentleman. He was as tall as Mary and
almost as broad shouldered. He was in
partnership with other manufacturers to
corner the spermaceti whale oil market.
Richard had been very generous with me,
bringing me books of poetry by Gray,
Dryden, Milton, and Pope.

Mary's mood was so infectious that I felt
giddy too. Dancing down the stairs, I
practically pirouetted toward the door. I
opened it, giving my deepest curtsy.

"Welcome, Sir Richard," I said, suppres-
sing a giggle.

Then I saw that Richard was not alone.
John Adams was with him! A rush of blood
warmed my cheeks.

"Oh, Mr. Adams," I stammered as Mary
came down the stairs. She helped the men off
with their coats, stowing them in the entry
closet under the stairs. I dropped, disgusted
with myself, onto the hard wooden bench
outside the library door.

It was surprising to me that John Adams
should cause me so much embarrassment. I
knew I would have laughed at my foolishness
had it been any other young man. As I looked
up at John Adams with his plump cheeks and

strong, stocky figure, my feelings toward
him puzzled me. He was the exact opposite of
the two men I loved and admired most, my
father and my uncle-cousin Dr. Cotton Tufts.
They were both tall, lean, and spare men.

My father came to the library door and
said, "Come into my study, John."

"I'll bring some apples," I said.

Placing the apples in a bowl, my thoughts
were still completely taken with John
Adams. Why, I wondered, did he make me
feel so shy? I had known him ever since I was
a little girl. He lived just four miles away on a
farm in Braintree. He had graduated from
Harvard, taught school, and now he was
getting started as a lawyer. There was
nothing about him that should make me
tongue-tied.

As I entered father's study with the bowl
of apples I wished I had worn something
prettier than the old brown calico.

"These are apples from a tree Father and I
planted together one day when I was a little
girl. I've nurtured the tree in our houseyard
myself," I said.

John Adams' eyes widened. I suppose he
was surprised because most girls weren't
interested in horticulture. Having heard that
he was interested in fruit trees and everything else on his farm, I thought our apple
tree worth mentioning. When I saw his
immediate interest, I knew why his friends
called him Farmer John.

John Adams came back again and again.
He always seemed to be calling on Father.
They had long discussions about politics and
Samuel Adams and James Otis who spoke
out against the Writs of Assistance in the
Supreme Court.

As spring came to Weymouth the talk of
England's injustices continued, but the
glorious New England green-up time lured
everyone away from serious thought and
took them outdoors.

One day Mary and Richard asked me and
John Adams to accompany them on a picnic.

"You're too delicate for a boat ride,"
Mother said. "I'm not sure . . ."

On that picnic Saturday morning I woke up
early with a quivering excitement. I slipped
downstairs to find Phoebe was already at the
storage porch preparing the picnic lunch. The
oaken tub was filled with bath water and
awaiting me. With bayberry soap and a white
flannel cloth I scrubbed myself glowingly
clean. Phoebe had my towel in the baking
oven to warm. I stood on the oval, wool,
braided rug just long enough to dry and then
draping the towel around myself, I made a
quick run through the dining room, to the
sitting room, and would have run upstairs
when I heard loud voices in the study.

I heard Mother ask, "Why are you so
friendly to John Adams?"

I stopped short in the hallway. This was
the first time I had ever heard my parents
discuss John Adams. Should I eavesdrop, I
wondered? My conscience told me "No!" My
curiosity told me "Stay!"

Father said, "It is time Nabby had friends
now that Mary is engaged."

Mother said, "He's the son of a farmer and
he's a lawyer. Lawyers are justly held in low
esteem. Their only purpose is to help
wrongdoers."

I ran up the stairs and almost collided with
Mary as she came down the stairs for her
bath.

"What's wrong?" Mary asked. "You're pale and your eyes are flashing like beacons from the lighthouse."

The words flowed from me. Poor Mary stood flabbergasted as I poured out my defense of John Adams to her.

I said, "Of course John comes from a long line of farmers. He's had a college education at Harvard where he distinguished himself. He's a fine Christian. His father wanted him to go into the church, but he had no leading of God. His friends knew his powers of argument were great and persuaded him that the law was his proper profession. To support himself while he was studying, he taught school. Mary, does this not prove him to be a serious, good young man?"

"Yes, yes," Mary cried, wide-eyed and startled.

"Mother doesn't want me to go with you and Richard," I went on. "I can't tell which she objects to more, Mr. Adams or the boat."

Mary put her hand on my arm. "I'll speak to Mother. I'll tell her you'll wear your wool stockings and your goloe-shoes to protect yourself from taking ill. It'll be all right. You'll see."

The men rowed the boat to Rainsford Island. Mary and I sat together in the bow. John Adams was quiet. He seemed to be enjoying the exercise. Richard Cranch talked a rhythm to the oar strokes. He talked mostly about cogwheels and pumps.

Soon they beached the boat and we spread Phoebe's picnic lunch on a flat boulder set on a circle of marsh rosemary. John lingered long over the chicken and cider and johnny-cake while Mary and Richard went in search of sea shells.

Finally John spread his coat on the bank and I sat down on his coat. Gulls cawed and screamed above us. The sea was beautiful that day. God's perfect creation. John seemed like a proper part of the scene, especially his eyes. They were like the sea. They were deep blue except when he was opposed to something. Then his eyes were gray like the clouds that hung over the water. His eyes looked almost purple when he was angry. A moody man, this John Adams. He was as moody as the sea.

He was talking about the law. Suddenly he turned and looked deep into my eyes. He said, "I admire the law, Miss Abigail Smith. Law is human reason. Law is justice. It guarantees our rights."

"Yes, I agree, Mr. Adams," I nodded. "And does it take all your time to study the law?"

"I have other pursuits as well," he said.

"What do you do with your time?" I asked.

His eyes grew big and blue as he said, "I gallant the girls."

I stared at him unbelievingly. I had never heard that John Adams was a man who enjoyed the company of many ladies. And then the humor of it struck me. Of course, it was well known that Mr. Adams had little time or interest in courting.

A laugh chortled in my throat. Then we both burst into loud and boisterous laughter.

"That wasn't true, you know," he said between laughs.

Soon Mary and Richard came back with their shells and turned back to the boat. A wind was whipping itself up from the south. John took off his coat and wrapped it around me.

It was the next evening when I learned from Richard that John had come down with a cold. I felt responsible since I had worn his coat. I decided to talk to Cousin Cotton. Cousin Cotton was really a double relative. He was an uncle by marriage on my mother's side and a blood cousin on my father's. He was Weymouth's doctor.

A bell tinkled as I opened his front door.

"Cousin Cotton," I greeted him.

His big lips parted into a pleasant smile as he looked up from his workbench where he was grinding herbs with a stone pestle. His kindly brown eyes focused on me as they adjusted to the flickering candlelight.

"Cousin, do you have a cure for a cold?" I asked.

"Who has a cold?"

"John Adams."

"John Adams!" Cousin Cotton's mouth gaped open.

"He was over-heated from rowing. He took his coat off when a wind came up and gave it to me."

"Well, well, well," laughed Cousin Cotton. "That's the first time I've ever heard anything gallant and romantic about John Adams!"

"What do you prescribe, Doctor?"

"Tell your Mr. Adams to go to bed for a day with a volume by Herodotus, strong beef broth, and a jug of Barbados rum. Between the three, nature will cure him."

"He's not *my* Mr. Adams. He will not take rum. He told me yesterday of an article he wrote against taverns and rum drinking," I told the doctor.

"Then I shall have to call on him and take

him some herb medicine," said Cousin
Cotton.

"Thank you," I said and left hurriedly
because I was becoming embarrassed by
Cousin Cotton's grin when he mentioned
John Adams.

On the following Sunday I saw John at
church and he seemed perfectly well. I hoped
he would talk to me, but he left church with
the Tuftses. It was a disappointment.

But perhaps he'd come to tea I consoled
myself. On Sunday tea was always served at
the Reverend Smith's parsonage. Usually
there were forty or more parishioners
attending. Father led beautiful devotions,
and Mother presided over the tea table with
pleasure.

Just as I had hoped, I saw John as he
approached our house. I had never seen him
so well dressed before. His wig was powdered and brushed and gathered neatly
behind his ears. He wore a white linen collar,
a coat and vest of wool adorned with
embossed buttons.

"Thank you, Miss Abigail," he said striding
up to me with strong even steps. "Thank you
for sending me that cold remedy."

"It is my expression of love of the Lord to
help the afflicted," I told him. "I am pleased
to help others in His name."

I saw John Adams frequently after that.
One day he asked me to marry him. I thought
I'd burst with excitement. But when he asked
permission to speak to Father alone, I saw
my mother's expression tighten. Her jaws
set into a straight thin line. She told me it
was time for me to retire.

What a restless night it was! Would Father

give his consent? Did Father not always say I must have a mind of my own? If that were so and I knew in my mind as well as in my heart that I loved John should I not insist that Father give his consent? I prayed fervently that the Lord would see fit to bless our union.

It was not until after breakfast the next morning that Father talked about his interview with John Adams. "He has asked permission to marry you, Abigail," Father said.

"He's only a lawyer," Mother said. "His father is only a country farmer."

"I consider him a brilliant young man," Father said. "I am convinced that he will do well with his future."

Then Father turned to me and asked, "How do you feel about John Adams, Abigail?"

"I love him," I said, and felt warm color come to my cheeks. My heart was pounding with happiness. Father was on my side. Father liked John!

"Then I shall tell John he may continue to call on you," Father said. He glanced at Mother as if to tell her that his word was final.

Mother raised her chin high. "There will be no talk of marriage for a long time," she said quietly but firmly. "Abigail isn't strong enough. And Mary must be married first."

Chapter VI

Mrs. John Adams

I tried to make up to John for all the coolness he met at my home. I wrote him letters when he was away riding the circuit of the courts.

All of Weymouth talked about my suitor. Phoebe said, "People is saying that you're courting below your station, Miss Nabby."

When John wasn't riding the circuit he came over from Braintree two evenings a week and on Saturday nights stayed with Cotton Tufts.

One day Father and I were alone in the study. Father said, "My dear, Abby. I have something to say to you. I know it is not easy to wait like this for the proper time for your wedding. But if your love is true you will wait. From a lifetime of reading Scripture I have come to believe that true love is God's will and therefore worth waiting for."

I felt the tears well up behind my eyelids as I said, "Thank you, Father. You have made the waiting a little easier." I trusted that the Lord knew best.

As the days went on I used them for preparing for the time when I would be Mrs. Adams. I learned to dip candle wicks and make soap from grease and wood ash. Mother helped me improve my technique of spinning flax and wool. Phoebe showed me how to make pickling fluids for purple cabbage, green walnuts, and fish. The making of rich fruit perserves was carefully learned. Tom showed me how to get quills for

pens. Father trained me in salting cod and smoking ham and venison.

In the fall I was caught up in the weeks of getting ready for Mary's wedding. Father's wedding sermon was based on Luke 10:42: "Mary hath chosen that good part, which shall not be taken away from her."

The wedding reception at the parsonage was one of the biggest Weymouth had ever seen. There were over a hundred Quincys, Nortons, and Smiths from just about every part of Massachusetts. And then, of course, there were the dear friends in the church's congregation and the deacons, elders and selectmen.

Phoebe and Tom were in charge of the eleven serving girls who brought in trays and trays of smoked meats and game birds.

John Adams came to the parsonage with Cotton Tufts. John and my cousin seemed to be spending the afternoon keeping out of

Mother's way, and trying to save Mary from being kidnapped by the young men of Weymouth.

"I have learned of the plot to steal Mary," John whispered in my ear as we stepped into the houseyard together.

I was not surprised for "Stealing the Bride" was a favorite game at Massachusetts weddings. If the young men got Mary to a neighboring tavern, Richard would have to pay the bill. Mary would not be free to go on her honeymoon until the next day.

"How did you learn of it?" I asked.

"I haven't time to tell you about that now. We must find Richard. You draw him aside and tell him to meet me by the apple tree," John said, looking scanningly about the grounds.

I hurried back inside and found Richard going into the room where all the gentlemen were gathering.

Pulling at his arm I whispered, "Richard, meet John by the apple tree in the house-yard. He knows of a plan to abduct Mary."

Richard shot me a grateful glance and slipped away toward the entry door.

Richard and Mary were safely on their way to their new home in Germantown when the last guests parted.

Mother came up to John who lingered on to the end of the reception. "Mr. Adams," Mother said. "I wish to thank you for foiling the plot to abduct Mary. Your efforts in my daughter's behalf are most appreciated."

John smiled. I knew he was thinking that maybe some day Mother would approve of him. He bowed ever so slightly and prepared to leave. I walked with him to where his horse was posted.

"When will I be going with you?" I asked, looking up into the clear blue eyes.

"I am hoping by February," John said as he mounted his horse and rode away.

But in February there was an outbreak of smallpox. Dr. Cotton Tufts said this epidemic looked as if it would be as bad as the one that had broken out in 1721, when more than half the population of Boston came down with the disease and many died.

It was while John and I were having dinner with Cousin Cotton and Aunt Lucy when Dr. Cotton Tufts made an announcement. "An epidemic in Boston could easily be carried to Weymouth and Braintree. We go to Boston often. We could bring the disease here. We must be inoculated. There are two private hospitals in Boston being opened and I suggest we take the full treatment."

"What about me?" I asked.

"Women don't get inoculated, Abby. Hospitals are only for men," Cousin Cotton explained.

John was frowning. "Riding circuit I need protection. Right now I have two cases which have to be settled. I could take the inoculation by the middle of February. How long does the treatment take?"

"About four weeks in the hospital. Two or three more weeks at home to gain back strength, seeing no one. Smallpox can be contagious even during its last days."

My hands lay quietly in my lap, but I was counting on my fingers how long it would be before I saw John again. John was looking up at the ceiling as if he was counting too. As our eyes met it was as if we were saying to each other, "It will be the middle of April before we see each other again."

Days wore by. I wrote to John and waited eagerly for his letters. He wrote his reaction to the inoculation: "a short shivering fit and a succeeding hot glowing fit, a want of appetite." As for the pox themselves he said in another letter: "about eight or ten. . .two of which are on my face, the rest scattered at random over my limbs and body."

One day just before John left Boston I was in my bedroom writing to him when Mother's soft knock at my door and her quiet entrance surprised me. Mother did not usually interrupt me when I was in my room.

"Tell Mr. Adams he has my good wishes for his safety," she said. This was the closest Mother had ever come to accepting John. It made me so happy I jumped up and threw my arms around her and kissing her exclaimed, "You are kind, Mother. I love you."

Mother smiled. "I love you too, dear. You must know what I do, I do out of love."

It was almost summer before John left his mother's house in Braintree. That first day, when he came to the parsonage, he was bursting with good health and vigor.

"Miss Adorable," he said to me, cupping my chin in his hand, "let's begin our wedding preparations at once. I'll select the heavy furniture in Boston for your approval and you get busy assembling whatever it is you feel you must have."

"What date did you have in mind, John?" I asked quietly though I felt boisterously happy.

"Late October would be suitable, I think," John said. "We'll have everything we need to make a start by then."

"Yes, John," I said.

It was almost three years since John had proposed marriage. And now with Mother's blessing, wedding plans were being made. Mother helped me get my pewter tableware, glasses, bowls, silver mugs, a spinning wheel, a skillet on legs, and irons and bellows.

John said it was hard to get furniture and other goods. Goods from England were not plentiful because England and the colonies were not on the best of terms. Parliament had passed the Sugar Act and the colonists did not like it. People in Massachusetts refused to buy anything grown or manufactured in England. It was difficult to buy brass and copper kettles because there were no good American made kettles.

But finally John and I had gathered enough goods for our start in life together and our wedding day, October 25, 1764, dawned bright as the fall foliage. I was twenty and John was twenty-nine.

We were married in the parlor of the parsonage. It was not the big wedding that Mary had. Relatives were not so impressed with John Adams the farmer's son as they had been with Richard Cranch the successful businessman of good family.

But the parlor was gay with autumn fruits and foliage. My heart sang a hymn of thanksgiving to the Lord for giving me John. I prayed God would bless our marriage.

I wore a red and white sprigged woolen dress and I had a bright new cloak for going away. John was in dark blue broadcloth and had a white satin waistcoat embroidered by his mother in gold thread with sprays of wheat.

Father performed the wedding service. His voice was never more vibrant than on that day.

When the wedding feast was over John lifted me on his big, brown mare. I rode with him toward our new home. Judah, the Negro servant Mother had loaned us, rode in a cart with the chest of linen and woolen goods that I had made.

"This is our home," John said when we came to a small house facing the high road in Braintree. We dismounted and walked to the green slope of Penn's Hill across the road.

"You can watch the sea from the top of this hill," he said. "On a clear day you can see a great distance—almost to Boston."

"Father told me that the original two-room cabin had been built on this spot in 1680," I said scanning the house and the countryside eagerly. Several additions had now been made to it. This was to be our home, our farm!

North of our house was another house which looked almost like it. It was the house where John had been born. John's mother and younger brothers, Peter and Elihu, lived there now. The two houses were almost alike. Both were slope-roofed cottages. They were built of clapboards which had turned grayish brown.

"I know I'll be happy here," I told John. As we walked into the house I was mentally arranging all my things. The house was built around a very large central chimney with huge fireplaces and deep ovens. There was a long sloping roof above the kitchen, and there was a narrow stairway to the upper floor.

"And I have a parlor and you have an office for your law clients!" I exclaimed happily.

In the days that followed I saw how much John loved his farm, a nine-acre tract of land. He did most of the work himself, though his law practice was growing and taking more and more of his time.

John's mother and I became good friends and we visited back and forth. I got on well

with his brothers too. Mary and Richard
lived near us now at Salem. Mount Wollaston
was a nice walk from our home. Grandma
Quincy was still my favorite and we had
many long talks. I did not lack for good
company.

Grandfather Quincy was occupied with the
new King George. He was a different type of
king from George II. This George III was
going to make his colonies contribute money
whether they liked it or not. He put a tax on
legal documents that had never been taxed
before. Massachusetts refused to pay unless
she was represented in Parliament. This new
king would not have colonists in Parliament
and the courts of Massachusetts were closed.

During all the trouble with England our
first child was born on July 14, 1765. We
named her Abigail. I was pleased that John
wanted that name. Now there was a new
little Nabby in our family. It pleased me too
when Father christened the baby and dedicated my child to the Lord.

"I remember a cold day in November when
I christened you," Father said. "Now I'm
going to christen another Abigail." His eyes
clouded over with memories as he went on.
"It was so cold that day we needed an Indian
tomahawk to crack the ice in the baptismal
font," he recalled. Then he brightened as he
said, "There'll be no need of such goings on
this hot day in July!"

As talk went on about the Stamp Act, I
remembered John once said that England
would not be able to hold on to her colonies if
they would ever unite against her. I wondered if the colonists would really ever be
angry enough to unite.

Not a single stamp was sold in America. In May 1766 the Stamp Act was repealed. John had spoken out against the Act and had written resolutions against it. The town of Boston had asked John to present a petition against the Act to the British governor in Massachusetts. All this activity was making John one of the most important men in the colony.

A little over a year later my beloved Grandfather Quincy died. It was the first loss of someone dear that I had ever known. Without my faith, knowing that Grandfather was with the Lord, I couldn't have taken my loss very well. "He that believeth on the Son hath everlasting life" (John 3:36) I reminded myself. I cried as I lay in my four-poster bed with my new baby. Just two days before my grandfather's death our first son was born, July 11, 1767. We named him John Quincy, in honor of Grandfather.

Chapter VII

Happenings In Boston

We had lived in Braintree for more than three years when John came into my kitchen one day. He sat at the table watching me stir the stew in the iron kettle. I knew he had something on his mind and was wondering how to tell me.

"John," I said, "do not worry about phrasing as if you were preparing a court case. Tell me simply what is on your mind."

"Very well," John said. "I think we should move to Boston."

"Boston?" I repeated. It had never crossed my mind that I would leave my little home in Braintree.

"My cousin, Sam Adams has advised it. He thinks my law practice would grow in Boston."

I looked at John's weary face. I realized that the ten-mile trip to Boston was much too much for him. Besides, I thought, John is becoming involved in the politics of Massachusetts and political happenings are taking place in Boston.

"Yes," I said. "I think Boston is where we must be."

"Then, Abby, I'll find a house to rent. When I have found a suitable place, we shall move."

At the end of April in 1768, we moved into a rented house in Brattle Square. It was in the busy part of the city. It was a good location for a lawyer. John's office was on the ground floor.

I missed all my dearly beloved visitors in Braintree but our home was not without callers. Sam Adams, a cousin of John's, came often. One day he said to me, "My whole interest is in politics, Abby. I know I've held only small offices, but John says I have a great influence with the working people."

"What John says is important to me too," I told him.

John Hancock came to our house often. He lived in a big stone mansion on Beacon Hill. My husband told me that when John Hancock's Aunt Lydia died he would be the richest man in New England.

John Hancock came one day, beautifully dressed as usual, but with a ferocious frown on his forehead.

"Parliament has passed the Townshend Act!" he cried.

"What does the Act mean to us?" I asked.

"It puts a tax on tea, glass, lead, paper, and painter's colors. This time, I fear, the king is determined to have the new law obeyed."

"Dear Father, in heaven," I prayed, "give us the strength to bear up under these injustices."

"Amen," added Mr. Hancock.

But in September the injustice became worse. At the wharf I saw an English ship bring two regiments of troops to Boston. The British soldiers in their bright, red uniforms were everywhere.

"They came to see that we pay them new taxes," one man grumbled to another as I walked by.

"Nobody in Boston's going to house the lobster backs," cried the other man.

What I overheard that day at the wharf came to pass. People refused to house the

British soldiers. Most of them were camped
on the Common, a grassy plot in town. The
Common was only three blocks away from
our home!

I awoke one morning with strange sounds
in my ears. It was the roll of drums and the
high notes of fifes. Then there was the
tramp, tramp, tramp of boots on the cobble-
stones. An officer yelled out commands.

I sat upright in bed. I could hardly stand
the sounds of the camp. I was physically
shaken.

During all this trouble my third child, little
Susannah, had died. Her death and the
presence of the British in Boston made me
yearn for our home in Braintree and the quiet
and security there. However, I never fal-
tered in my belief in God's wisdom. I knew
He directed our steps.

One night in March John went to a political
meeting at the South End of Boston. Our two

children were snuggled in their beds. Suddenly church bells began to ring.

A cry came from the street: "Town-born turn out!"

It was the cry of the Sons of Liberty, a secret society organized to fight against the unfair laws.

Running to the window, panic gripping my throat, I leaned out. I called out to the men and women running toward King Street.

"What is happening? Where is everyone running to?"

The children heard me and ran in fright to my side. They hugged my skirts, looking up at me wide-eyed and trembling. I cuddled them to me.

There was the unmistakable sound of guns firing. My thoughts were with John. Where was he? Was he safe? "Dear Lord," I prayed, "watch over him."

Sukey, the maid, and Jonah, the house boy, rushed into the room.

"Mistress Adams, Mistress Adams," they called out. "Everyone is going to King Street. It must be bad!"

"Go, Jonah, go!" I commanded. "Find your master. Find out what has happened and hurry back with the news!"

"I want my Papa. Is my Papa hurt? I want my Papa!" little John Quincy sobbed into my skirts. But Nabby's crying almost drowned out his voice.

A stiff wind blew cold into the room as I looked out the window drawing the children to me. I glimpsed a familiar figure running toward the house. It was John!

The children still clinging to me we hurried to the front door.

"Praise be to God you're safe!" I cried.

As John removed his cloak he kissed the children then nodded to Sukey to take them to bed, his words tumbling out in excited rapidity. "I was at the meeting when we heard the church bells. We thought it was a fire alarm and ran out into the street with fire buckets. We followed the crowds of people to King Street. When we got there the snow was red with blood and bodies were being carried away."

"What happened?" I asked wide-eyed with amazement.

"Boys and men were throwing snowballs. They jeered at one sentry in front of the Town House. Someone flung a stone. Others followed. Somebody went for the officer in charge, a Captain Preston, who was in the warehouse across the street."

"That should have quieted the crowd," I said.

"It did not," John went on in frantic haste. "Preston sent a corporal and seven men, and then he came himself."

"Did the crowd back away then?" I wanted to know.

"Indeed they didn't," replied John. "They continued to call the soldiers Bloodybacks and Lobsters. Then young Henry Knox, the bookseller's assistant, asked Captain Preston if he was going to give the order to fire. Preston said no, not if he could restore order without it.

"Good for Captain Preston!" I said.

John went on. "Someone knocked a soldier's weapon out of his hand, at the same time striking him over the head with a wooden club. The soldier pulled the trigger. Other soldiers did the same automatically."

I stood in shocked silence. John's story sent shivers of fear through me.

"Each shot found a target. Five people died. Eight were wounded."

We walked to the kitchen where I brewed tea. We heard English soldiers walking past the house on patrol duty. But we were English too. How impossible this all seemed! Bells continued to ring. Drums thudded. People in the streets were calling, "Townsfolk, turn out! To arms!"

There was a knock at the door. It was a selectman. "Come with us, John," he said. "We are going to Stingy Tommy Hutchinson's and demand that he order all soldiers back to barracks."

John did not return until dawn. Before he dropped into exhausted sleep he told me that Captain Preston had been arrested along with those of his men who had fired. They would stand trial in Boston.

Months dragged by as John and Josiah Quincy worked on almost nothing else but the case of the British soldiers. It was August before the case was tried.

The day the soldiers were being tried I rose early. I wanted to be in the courtroom when John presented this unpopular case. I knew people would brand him an English sympathizer and call him "Tory." I admired my husband for taking the side of right as he knew it to be.

The courtroom was filled with people. This was an important case. There were four judges on the bench, all wearing the official full wigs and red robes.

John was in his black robe and he too wore a full white wig. His blue eyes were an overcast gray as he began pleading his case. I

knew he had questioned ninety-six witnesses including Patrick Carr. Patrick had died, but before he died he had given a statement to his doctor which John used in court.

Patrick had told the doctor, "I bear no grudge. The soldiers only did their duty. They fired in self-defense."

My heart swelled with pride as I listened to John present the facts in his logical way.

The trial lasted for eleven days and then the verdict was passed down—"not guilty" for Captain Preston and six of the soldiers. The two soldiers who fired first were found guilty of manslaughter and branded on their hands for punishment.

After the trial was over the soldiers crowded around John. One soldier said, "You are a brave and honest man. We owe our lives to you."

Once again my heart filled with love and pride. I hoped that now the strife would be over between England and the colonies. But there was more to come, much more.

By 1773 the Townshend Acts had been repealed and taxes had been lifted on all imported goods except tea. I breathed easier and busied myself with our new babies, Charles, who had been born to us in May of 1770, and Thomas in September of 1772.

We returned to Braintree for John was exhausted by his work in Boston. John rode the court circuit again. It was a forty-mile circuit and he was gone for many days at a time. But I contented myself with writing letters to John and visiting Mercy Otis Warren, my friend at Plymouth; enjoying stimulating conversations and tea in her gambrel-roofed house among the trees.

Such enjoyment was soon curtailed by that baneful weed, tea. Because of the Whigs' fury over a tax on tea John was asked once more to return to Boston.

This time John bought a house on Queen Street. I settled the family in while John flung himself into arguments over that troublesome brew.

When November came a ship named *Dartmouth* sailed into Boston Harbor with a cargo of tea. I knew there was to be trouble. I sought strength for the days to come. The only comfort for me was the Scripture. I read over and over again, "Draw nigh to God, and he will draw nigh to you" (James 4:8), and "My help cometh from the Lord, which made heaven and earth" (Psalm 121:2).

The trouble I feared drew closer. One day John told me, "The colonists will not drink tea. It's not the price to which they object, but being taxed without their consent."

Every night John took his turn as guard at Griffin's Wharf. Governor Hutchinson had told Mr. Rotch, the captain of the *Dartmouth* that the ship could not leave the harbor unless it was unloaded. If it was not unloaded in twenty days, the tea would be seized by the custom officers.

"They will not land the tea!" John exclaimed, pounding the desk with his doubled-up fist.

But one night he came home weary and discouraged-looking. "Abby," he said, "now there are two other ships, carrying cargos of tea, tied up at Griffin's Wharf."

On December 16 when I should have been gay with the holiday spirit, a heavy doom seemed to fill me. I tried to think about the blessing of the Savior's birth. John was away on a business trip.

During his absence my cousin, Will Smith, came to call. He grinned as I opened the door. "I've come to borrow your old red blanket, Cousin Abigail," he said.

"You are welcome to the blanket, Cousin Smith," I said, trying not to show how startled I was, "but may I ask why you need it?"

"We're going to have a salt-water tea party," was all the explanation he gave. He grabbed the red blanket and called over his shoulder, "I'm off now to the Green Tavern."

I had to know what was happening. I called

to Jonah who had just entered the back door. "Jonah!" I called, "what is going on?"

"Everybody's going to Griffin's Wharf," Jonah said in a falsettoed voice due to his excitement. "Sam Adams has given the word. People say Boston Harbor will be a teapot tonight!" I could not stay home. I had to see what was happening.

Jonah pushed a path for me as we made our way into the crowded streets. At the wharf, Jonah found a cask on which I could stand. It was possible to see because dozens of pine torches burned brightly. The wharf was stirring with people. There were three groups of men and boys wearing blankets, their faces covered with fireplace soot. They carried axes over their shoulders and had colorful feathers in their hair. They were taking their places near each ship. There was the flame of freedom in their eyes. I felt for their cause and yet I feared for them. In the midst of the tumult I bowed my head and said silently, "Lord, dismiss them with thy blessing. Give them hope and comfort from above."

"Me know you!" called each person as he joined the group.

"That must be the password," I told Jonah.

The full moon shone down from a clear December sky. The ships and their riggings were clearly visible. Men made their way up the gangway of each ship; the *Eleanor*, the *Beaver*, and the *Dartmouth*. The crowd watched in hushed silence. I saw the captains come on the decks. From their movements it looked as if they were giving over their keys. The chests of tea were brought to the decks. Sounds of splintering wood filled the damp air. Then there was one splash after

another, whoosh! Broken chests were drift-
ing on the water. The smell of tea wafted in
from the harbor. Tea leaves drifted with the
current.

Finally, one by one, the men came down
the gangplank. A fife began to play. Drum
rolls began as the men started to march to
the Town House. The crowd watched quietly.

Jonah and I trailed behind the thinning
crowd. I was too disturbed to sleep that
night. It was with great relief that I greeted
John on his return from his business trip the
next day. As soon as I told him about the "tea
party" which Jonah and I had watched, he
went to Sam Adams's house to get the full
details.

John soon returned with the news. "The
tide was low," he said. "There is tea along the
shore as far as Dorchester."

"How much tea was destroyed?" I asked.

"Sam says about three hundred chests,
about eighteen thousand pounds."

"Who will pay the cost of this Indian
caper?" I asked.

John looked down and gripped his hands
together as he spoke seriously, "Boston will.
And perhaps the 'price' will spread far
beyond Boston."

Chapter VIII

Pewter And Bullets

It was May when Boston learned of her punishment. Governor Hutchinson returned to England and General Gage was appointed Royal Governor Gage. The first act of the new governor was to close the port of Boston. Boston's door, the Atlantic Ocean, was closed and locked!

Sailors, merchants, field hands and shipbuilders were idle. Everyone began calling the new laws the "Intolerable Acts."

"John," I said to my husband over breakfast, "your law practice depends on all these people who are now out of work."

"True, Abigail," he nodded. "We can afford to live here no longer. We will have to move back to Braintree."

A lump rose in my throat as I realized we

must leave the Boston home to whatever
would happen to it.

At Braintree we heard that the other
colonies were in sympathy with Boston. They
deeply resented what England was doing. "If
it can happen in Boston, it can happen here,"
their leaders complained.

John left again to meet with others at
Salem. There John wrote:

> *The unhappy differences between Great
> Britain and the American Colonies were
> debated. The thirteen colonies are to meet
> in a Continental Congress in Philadelphia.*

The Massachusetts delegates were chosen:
Thomas Cushing, Samuel Adams, Robert
Treat Paine, and John Adams.

On our farm John and I walked together
before he was to leave. We walked through
the cornfields, the barley rows, the orchards,
the dairy, and the pens. He gave instructions
as to how I was to run the farm while he was
gone. We went to church and prayed. Then I
rode into town with him and stood in the
crowd as he and the other delegates climbed
into the stagecoach.

Although I did not hear from John for five
weeks, the newspapers did write of his safe
arrival.

At last a letter came. They were greeted
with enthusiasm everywhere they went,
John said.

But I was troubled. The summer was hot
and dry. Crops faded. Since the cows did not
have enough grass, the milk supply
dwindled.

Dressing, feeding, and playing with the
four children helped me forget my fears and
troubles. And I became their teacher. We

read the Bible together constantly. The children and I found great hope in the Holy Book.

I helped the men on the farm and did most of the cooking even though I had two servant girls. There was always butter to be churned, candles to be made, and spinning and weaving to be done.

John returned a troubled man. Then in April a horseman came to our house after midnight and told us: "The sexton of Christ Church in Boston has hung two lanterns in the steeple to warn everyone that the British regulars are coming by sea. Paul Revere has mounted a fast horse and ridden to Lexington. William Dawes has gotten by the sentry at the Neck. Church bells have sent other riders along the coast."

"What has happened? What could have happened?" I asked John over and over again.

"I'll ride to Concord and find out," John said when he too could no longer tolerate the suspense.

Soon John returned with the news. "On the eighteenth of April," John said, "General Gage sent troops to seize the powder the people had collected at Concord and to arrest the traitor leaders. Paul Revere learned of these plans and galloped ahead of the British and warned the people."

"How brave of him!" I exclaimed.

"When the British reached Lexington," John went on, "they found a small company of minutemen on the village green headed by Captain Parker. When the minutemen stood their ground and would not disperse, the British fired a volley of musket shots leaving

eight of the patriots dead or dying on the
green. Reaching Concord the British destroyed the powder, then started the long
march back to Boston. They were fired on
from behind stone walls and apple trees. The
colonial militia, aroused for miles around,
closed in on Boston 16,000 strong and held
Gage in his own capital."

Tears sprang to my eyes. "May God
forgive our trespasses as we forgive those
who trespass against us," I whispered softly.

"There is no hope that the English or the
Patriots will forgive each other now," John
said bowing his head sadly. "King George
will not listen to our petitions after these
happenings. I shall have to leave for
Philadelphia."

When John left this time for Philadelphia
he held me close and said, "In case of real
danger, flee to the woods with our children."

John had been gone a few days when one
morning I woke with a start. I crept out of
bed and tiptoed to the window. I heard again
the sound which had awakened me before. It
was a warning drum! Away, over the hill, I
heard the meetinghouse bell ringing. "Could
it be that the British were coming to
Braintree?" I wondered.

After dressing quickly, I called the maids,
Susie and Patty.

"Dress the children. There's trouble," I
commanded.

"Why are we getting up this early?" the
children wanted to know.

"Eat your breakfast, children," I answered
as calmly as I could. "We have a busy day
ahead."

While the children ate I ran to the barn and

told one of the farm hands to find out why the meetinghouse bell had been rung.

When he came back he was breathless from the long hard run. Between short breaths he panted, "The English are coming! Everyone is running for their lives. Our neighbors are piling their belongings into carts and getting away from here."

I looked out the window. The road was jammed with carts and wagons piled high with furniture, pots and pans, and bedding. People were sitting on top of their belongings or hanging on the sides of their wagons. Horses were straining under their heavy burdens.

"Run!" they called out to me. "The British are coming!"

The maids cowered in the corner of the kitchen. The children left their places at the table, their food half eaten. They clung to me. Charles and Tommy began to cry.

The wagons, the frightened children, the shouting, all brought back memories of that night in Weymouth when the meetinghouse burned down. I remembered how frightened Mary and I had been. I remembered how mother's quiet and composure had calmed us and made us feel safe. Now it was my duty to help my children over this frightening experience. "Father, please be with me," I prayed.

Walking unhurriedly to the kitchen table I said as calmly as I could, "We'll stay here in the safety of our home. There are no British soldiers here. The minutemen may be coming soon. They will be needing breakfast. We should have food ready for them, shouldn't we? Johnny, help the men put up the tables.

Nabby, get the bowls and spoons on the
tables. Tommy and Charlie, get water from
the well for coffee." God gave me the
strength.

Susie and Patty came out of the corner.
They got the largest kettles and slung them
on the cranes over the fire. The children
hurried to do their assigned chores. They
were less afraid in their busyness than they
would have been sitting in wait for something
to happen.

Something did happen. The minutemen did
come. When they saw all the food we were
preparing for them, they looked as if they
couldn't believe their own eyes.

"You haven't run away!" one of the men
said in wonder.

The men were hungry. They accepted the
food gratefully. They ate quickly and were
ready to leave when one of the men said, "I
wish we had some pewter like those spoons
you have hanging on the wall, Mrs. Adams.
Our men would almost give their ears for as
much as you have there."

I stared at my spoons for a moment. How
carefully I had chosen them before John and I
were married. Now they had a more
important use. Freedom and the God-given
rights of the people were more important
than pewter. I walked to the fireplace and
unhooked the long spoons and other utensils I
had hung there. I opened the cupboard
drawers and took out handfuls of tableware.

"You may have all my pewter," I told the
men.

"You are a good friend to the just cause of
the Patriots," one man said.

The men put the big iron soup kettle on the

logs. I threw the pewter into it. With a stirring rod I pushed the pewter down into the kettle.

"When the pewter has melted, make your bullets," I told them.

The men quickly made their bullets from the liquid and were soon on their way to meet the British.

The months wore on. A few letters from John came through from Philadelphia. John was impatient with the Congress. He wrote that the Congress was "as slow as snails."

I wrote an account of our life to John:

Soldiers come for lodging, for breakfast, for supper, for drink, etc. Sometimes refugees from Boston seek asylum for the day, a night, a week. You can hardly imagine how we live; yet . . .

"To the houseless child of want,
Our doors are open still;
And though our portions are but scant,
We give them with good will."

I wish you were nearer to us. We know not what a day will bring forth, nor what distress one hour may throw us into.

I am with the tenderest regard,

Your Portia

The maids told me that word about my pewter and about feeding and housing the needy had spread up and down the coast. People say, "She's the only one who didn't run away. She's a heroine."

I was very humbled by this praise. I felt I had merely observed the opportunity to help. I had faith that God would help the righteous.

Early on the morning of June 17 I was awakened by what sounded like thunder. Looking out the window I could see no sign of a storm. I ran to wake Johnny and Nabby.

"Johnny, run and get the spyglass, please, and Nabby, stay close to the children," I said. A wild explosion shook the house.

Nabby and Johnny's eyes were wide with fear and wonder. They stood motionless, looking at me for an explanation.

"Johnny," I explained, "you and I are going to the top of Penn's Hill.

Penn's Hill was a short distance from our home. It was one of several hills which overlooked Boston.

Cannons fired over our cornfield. The house shook and the dishes rattled in the cupboard. The windowpanes rattled as if they would burst out of their frames.

Taking Johnny's hand we climbed together to the top of Penn's Hill. We had a clear view of the town of Boston and the ocean to the east. North of Boston lay Charlestown. Breed's Hill and Bunker Hill were beyond.

Looking through the spyglass I realized that during the night the Americans had

fortified these hills for there were walls of
dirt with guns sticking out. Even though we
were ten miles away the spyglass brought it
all very close.

There was another tumultuous sound like
the one which had awakened me. It came
from the ships.

"Look, Mother," Johnny said, pointing to
the ships, "I see red flashes from the ships
and there are puffs of smoke."

My hands trembled so that I could no
longer hold the spyglass. Johnny took it from
me and looked through. He stood very close
to me. Then he too dropped the spyglass and
putting both arms around me asked, "Is this
a battle, Mother?"

"Yes, Johnny," I answered.

The guns from the ships fired all morning.
The Americans had taken position on Breed's
Hill, which was closer to the city than Bunker
Hill.

The sun was high in the sky when the
British commander in Boston sent his
soldiers to attack. The British were forced to
retreat.

Johnny and I made our way back to the
house and stayed just long enough to see that
the children were all right.

In the afternoon Johnny and I returned to
Penn's Hill. We saw the British row across
the water and attack the Americans for the
second time. The Americans fired many
times. The British retreated. The red coats of
the dead and dying men made bright spots of
color all over the hillside. It was a sad sight.

"Johnny," I said sadly, "please bow your
head for these fallen men." We prayed, "The
grace of the Lord Jesus Christ, and the love
of God, and the communion of the Holy

Ghost, be with you all." Prayer was too late for many soldiers.

When the British attacked the third time the Americans did not fire back. The Americans were driven off. The noise ceased.

Taking Johnny's hand I led him down Penn's Hill.

Back in Philadelphia John did not know of the Battle of Bunker Hill, and the letter he wrote was full of good cheer.

I can now inform you that Congress has made a choice of the modest and brave George Washington to be general of the American army. He is to report as soon as possible to the camp before Boston. The liberties of America depend upon him in a great degree.

I smiled with satisfaction. I knew it was John who had proposed George Washington's name.

John wrote again after receiving some Boston battle news. He told me about the Psalm reading and prayer Rev. Duché had given the Congress.

You must remember this was the morning after we heard the horrible rumor of the cannonade of Boston. I never saw a greater effect upon an audience. It seemed as if heaven had ordained that psalm [thirty-fifth] to be read on that morning. After this Mr. Duché unexpectedly to everybody struck out into an extemporary prayer . . . for America, for the Congress, for the province of Massachusetts Bay, and especially the town of Boston . . . Washington was kneeling, and Henry, and Randolph, and Rutledge, and Lee, and Jay, and by their sides there stood, bowed in reverence, the Puritan patriots of New England.

George Washington came to Watertown, near Boston, on July 2, 1775. The next day he took command of the New England militia. Everyone went to get a glimpse of this new Commander on whom so much depended.

I too was anxious to see this Virginia squire who was a planter and a slave owner. Besides, he was one of John's favorites. I held with John that this surely was the leader who was needed so very much.

I saw him the day after his arrival. He was riding his horse down the street. He wore a blue coat with buff facings and buff colored breeches. This was the new uniform of the Continentals. He wore a sword at his side, a cockaded hat on his head, and the markings of his rank on his epaulets.

There was a reception for Washington. I felt fortunate to be invited. As I entered the room and was guided to where General Washington was standing, I curtsied in my very best Grandmother-Quincy fashion.

General George Washington impressed me greatly as we spoke of John and his work in Philadelphia. We both spoke of what we hoped for the colonies.

As I returned home after the reception, lines from Dryden came to me. They seemed to apply directly to the man I had just met.

Mark his majestic fabric! He's a temple,
Sacred by birth, and built by hands divine;
His soul's the deity that lodges there;
Nor is the pile unworthy of the god!

Chapter IX

Independence

Boston was free, but not the thirteen colonies. General Washington moved his army to New York. He was sure the British would attack there next.

Late in March I wrote John a long letter:

I long to hear that you have declared independency. And, by the way, in the new code of laws which I suppose it will be necessary for you to make, I desire you would remember the ladies. Be more generous and favorable to them than your ancestors.

When the letter was sent I wondered if

John or any of the new lawmakers would actually consider women and their rights in the laws of the united thirteen colonies.

But matters of state did not concern me long. An epidemic broke out. It was not smallpox this time. It was dysentery.

John's brother, Elihu, was one of the first to come down with the malady. I hurried to my dear mother-in-law's side. The older woman was weary from nursing. Day and night I tended Elihu. He grew weak. I dreaded to tell John the fatal news. Elihu was dead.

When I returned home I heard a groaning from the barn. I ran as fast as I could to see who was in such pain. It was Isaac, my own stableman. I helped him to the house.

Soon I became sick too with the horrid disease. The new doctor came and bled Isaac. I prayed constantly.

Patty, the maid became sick. I wasn't well myself, but I knew I had to help the others as I could. With all my dwindling strength I tried to save Patty. I could not. She died.

I reminded myself of Romans 8:18: "For I reckon that the sufferings of the present time are not worthy to be compared with the glory which shall be revealed in us."

Tommy was growing more pale every day. I knew my child would be next. I prayed fervently beside Tommy.

Mother had tried to help administer to the sick and word came that she had taken the disease and died.

My heart was bursting with grief! But gradually with God's help my grief became bearable.

Finally the epidemic ended. I was thankful to God that my children were all safe.

The following June, John was on a committee to write a Declaration of Independence. Toward the middle of July, I received a letter from John which made my senses reel. The thirteen colonies were to be united. They were to be a nation. The nation was to be called the United States of America. John wrote that he believed the day of the uniting of the states was the most important day in the history of America. I called the children and read his letter to them.

It will be celebrated by succeeding generations as the great anniversary festival. It ought to be solemnized with pomp and parade, with game, bells, and bonfires from one end of the continent to the other, from this time forward forevermore.

The children jumped up and down in their excitement. I hurried outside and rang the farm bell. The children followed me and joined hands in a circle and romped around and around in their glee.

Then I said: "Come, children, let us go back into the house." This was a time to remember God—His care and blessings. We all knelt to pray for God's guidance for our new nation.

With John away the farm work weighed heavily on me. Farm workers were scarce because nearly all the men had joined the army.

Then there was the children's education to see to. The schoolmasters marched off to the army saying, "War's begun, school's done."

I instructed the children myself. I taught Latin and French to Nabby and Johnny, and I taught Charles and Tommy to read and write. But the Bible was the most important

book in teaching the children faith in God and
concepts of right and wrong.

The war went on. Supplies were short and
there was little or no money. One day my son
John Quincy came to me.

"Mother," he said. "I have heard that there
is a shortage of post-riders. I have just come
from General James Warren who told me it is
true. The men are all gone to war."

"But, Johnny," I protested, "you are only
nine years old!"

"But I can ride, Mother," Johnny insisted.
"General Warren says I can carry the mail
between here and Boston if I have your
permission."

I looked at my son. So small for his age! His
legs did not look long enough to stretch over
a horse that would be carrying saddlebags.
He was so persistent and anxious to help!

I said: "Yes, you may be a post-rider,
Johnny."

We learned, by post, that Benjamin
Franklin had been sent to France to ask that
nation to help our new nation. Arthur Lee
and Silas Deane were with Franklin.

Johnny rode the post every day. He rode
to Boston to pick up what riders brought in
from Philadelphia and elsewhere.

We began to think John would never come
home again. Then one day in August Johnny
brought a letter which said John was coming
home! He said he needed a horse. Our own
horse was lame. Father offered to send his
horse for John. We were bustling in prepara-
tion of the long awaited visit when another
dispatch from John said he had to put off his
visit again because battles had started
around New York. The Americans were

losing. But John was working to build a better army.

At last, in October another letter from John came. He was indeed coming! Johnny, Charles, and Tommy let out Indian war whoops. Every day was happier than the day before.

Johnny wished he did not have to ride the post while his father was home. But Johnny was constant in his job. One cold day in January Johnny came galloping home on his big bay horse.

John had arrived while Johnny was riding post and ran out to meet him. Johnny jumped off the bay into his father's arms. He was trembling and obviously excited.

John took the saddlebags and with an arm around our stammering Johnny led him to the kitchen fire.

Johnny drew a big, red-sealed letter from one of the bags and gave it to his father. Johnny's hands shook and he was trying to blurt out the news.

As my husband read the letter I saw his eyes change from blue to gray and then to clear blue again. Happiness and delight brightened his face like the sun sparkling on the sea after a storm.

"God be praised!" shouted my husband, actually doing a jig. "General Washington crossed the Delaware on Christmas night and overcame the Hessians!"

It seemed to me now, in the winter of 1777, after four years of distinguished service for the Continental Congress, that John would be free to take up his law practice again. But it was a vain hope. Congress called John to replace Silas Deane as a member of the commission to France.

"We shall all go with you, John!" I exclaimed happily.

"I shall ride to Boston and investigate what it would necessitate to take my family," John said.

When he returned he was tired. His eyes were clouded.

"John," I asked, "is it possible for us to come with you to France?"

"There are difficulties," he replied stretching his legs out toward the fire. "These are war times. There is a possibility that we may be captured. If that should happen the English would try me for treason and execute me. I shudder to think what would happen to my wife and children."

There was a long silence. Then John said, "Johnny has his heart set on coming with me."

"Not Johnny!" I cried. I gulped to hold back the sob that rose in my throat. How could I get along without my eldest? Johnny did so many things for me besides being the post-rider. It was Johnny I always turned to when I needed company and understanding when things were going badly. He was an excellent companion for the other three children. Little Nabby loved him so dearly. How she would miss him!

John cleared his throat as if reluctant to break into my thinking. Then he said, "As you know, Abby, the chance for a good education is limited in the colonies. There are great advantages to the education that is offered in Europe."

"But he's only ten! I shall think about it," I said sadly.

The next morning Johnny came to me, his turned up face looking at me pleadingly,

"Mother, you will let me go with Father, won't you?" he asked. "I could help Father. And Mother, I could learn. It is difficult to get a good education here. You've said so yourself many times."

I turned my full gaze on him as he watched me with silent, big eyes.

"Yes, Johnny, you can go," I said. Then I hastily turned and left the room lest I become emotional.

I thought of the words from James 5:16 "The effectual fervent prayer of a righteous man availeth much." And I prayed fervently for my two dear ones who would soon be leaving on a dangerous journey.

Three months later, from the top of Penn's Hill, I watched my two men leave from the landing at Mount Wollaston.

The next day my uncle, Norton Quincy gave me a letter Johnny had written just before he went on board the ship.

My uncle said, "The last thing Johnny said was, 'Give my love to Mamma.' "

I tried not to weep, but tears stung my eyes.

Six months passed before I had a letter from John, but through the *Boston Gazette* I found out that John and Johnny had landed safely in France.

In December I got two letters. John had written, but his other letters had been lost at sea. I learned that the voyage had taken months. They had been chased by British ships, and saved by a hurricane, then almost destroyed by it. I read they had been fired on and had fired back. Johnny had been unafraid and thrilled by it all.

I wrote long letters to Johnny telling him to study people and places and to ask about

what he saw. I told him to use his intelligence
for the benefit of himself and for his country's
future. I asked him to make friends; and
above all, to learn. I told Johnny the world
was his schoolroom.

John and Johnny were away for a year and
a half. One sunny August morning in 1779 a
coach drew up to our home in Braintree. John
and Johnny climbed out. The children
crowded around them and such talking and
laughing and hugging as went on!

"My little boy has become a man," I
thought as I held my son close, very close. He
was taller and even more serious than before.

"John Quincy learned to speak French like
a native," John said. "Youth is the only time
to learn a language."

That was a cue for the children, and
Johnny spent the rest of the day granting
their requests to "say something in French."

Once again our joyous reunion was cut
short for in three months Congress gave
John a new appointment. He was asked to
join Franklin in Europe to work on a peace
treaty. This time he took nine-year-old
Charles with him as well as Johnny.

But Charles was homesick. In January
1782 Charles came home with an officer of the
United States Navy. Johnny had stayed. He
had gone to Russia to be secretary to Francis
Dana, the first minister to Russia from the
United States.

"If you had known that Mr. Adams would
be away so long, would you have consented
to let him go?" a friend asked me one day.

"If I had known Mr. Adams would
accomplish what he did, I would have
endured his absence for three more years," I
told her.

Then a letter came from John. He was not coming home as I expected. Now he had been appointed to make commercial treaties with the countries of Europe. But there was a high note in his letter. John said he would not accept the appointment unless his wife and daughter could join him in Europe.

He wrote, "If you and Nabby were with me I could keep up my spirits. . ."

Eighteen-year-old Nabby was excited at the prospect of seeing her father and seeing Europe. John was making arrangements. We got caretakers for the farm and house in Braintree. Charles and Thomas were sent to live with my younger sister, Betsy. With two servants, John and Esther Briesler, we boarded the ship *Active* on June 20, 1784.

Chapter X

Citizen Of The World

It took thirty days to get from Boston to England. When I saw the *Active*, on which I was to sail lying in Boston Harbor, I had misgivings. I was remembering back to my childhood when I had visited Uncle Isaac's ship. The seasickness I felt on board that ship in just a few hours would be possible to feel again on this ship—for days and days.

The *Active* was riding steady on her ropes, but she seemed very small to be crossing the vast ocean. Nabby and I were escorted up the gangplank by the captain, Captain Lyde, and a Scotsman, Mr. Green. Then a mere lad showed us down a narrow stairway as steep as ours at Braintree. He nodded to a door, "Your stateroom, ladies," he said.

The stateroom was eight feet wide with two bunks on either side. The bunks were a mere three feet wide which left only two feet of empty space. There was a small window, but it opened to another part of the ship, not the sea. The ugly smell coming through was of cooking grease.

"The men's quarters are in the dining room too," the lad told us before he left.

"Well," said Nabby, looking at our stateroom with a practical eye, "there's a bunk for you and for me, and one for Esther. We can use the fourth one to lay out some of our things."

"Our trunks won't fit in here," I said. "They'll have to stay outside."

Esther wasn't saying anything. The poor young thing was turning yellow, and she was moaning already as the ship barely rocked.

"Poor Esther," I said. "She's seasick and we're still in Brattle Square! Come, Nabby, let's go on deck and watch the sailing."

On deck the sailors were casting off ropes. The Captain was shouting orders. The sails were raised and snapped in the wind.

The ship moved northward. The fresh, warm, June breeze cooled our faces as we watched Boston getting smaller and smaller on the horizon.

Two hours later the captain asked us to return to our stateroom and prepare ourselves for seasickness.

When we got back to our stateroom we saw that Esther had already been sick. A strange feeling stirred our stomachs. We put on our special oilcloth wrap-arounds and became sick ourselves.

Nabby raised once that night saying, "There is a Dr. Clark on board. Should I try to find him?"

"No," I said. "He'll be busy with others. There is nothing much he can do for us. We must suffer this out, Nabby."

Esther continued retching. Poor Esther hung for hours with her head over the side of the bunk.

The next morning she raised her head and looking up at me from her pitiable position said, "Mrs. Adams, would you please ask them to throw me overboard. I'm going to turn inside out anyway. I'd rather be dead."

Briesler and two stewards found an empty bunk elswhere for Esther. They carried her off like a sack of produce on Uncle Isaac's wharf. Briesler scrubbed the stateroom, and then got seasick himself.

For the next days and nights I held on to the sides of the bunk to keep from falling out.

Still I was grateful for the strong winds which were blowing me closer to John.

Finally I was able to crawl up on deck. But the wind was so cold, I couldn't stay there long.

After being at sea eight days the sea was calm. When I awoke that morning Esther was busying herself in our stateroom. She looked pale but she was smiling.

"Esther!" I exclaimed. "It is good to see you on your feet!"

"I have clean undergarments for you," Esther said. "I've fetched water too. I'll get your soap now from the other bunk."

At noon we all went to the galley for a meal. Instead of eating I sat and watched in disgust. There were not enough knives or cups. There was a leg of pork and roasted fowl. Twenty minutes later beef was brought in. Then there was cake. When everyone had eaten potatoes were served. When the pail of milk was brought in and I saw how dirty the pail was, I could keep silent no longer.

"I'm surprised you haven't all been poisoned by now," I told the passengers. "Let me have that pail. I'll scrub it myself."

When I returned with the pail everyone clapped, led by Dr. Clark.

After a month of sailing the captain ordered a sounding. The sailors let down chains to find the depth of the water. They found bottom at fifty-five fathoms. With a good wind we would be in sight of land in a day or two. But we had a windless day and floated becalmed.

The next morning we saw the cliffs of Dover in England. It was raining hard, but Nabby and I felt bright sunshine in our souls.

At last we were to be united with John and Johnny! My greatest desire!

Nabby said, "Delight thyself also in the Lord; and he shall give thee the desires of thine heart" (Psalm 37:4).

I was so excited I had to lean against the ship's railing to steady myself.

Captain Lyde told us the *Active* would be in the Channel a week before she could make it up the river. We were to land at Deal.

Finally the day to land came, and we were wrapped in oilskins and lowered from the ship into a ferry. When we reached land we still had to make a seventy-mile trip in mail coaches to London.

By evening we were at Low's Hotel in Covent Garden. There was no John to greet us.

London was bigger and more beautiful than I had pictured it. The houses looked orderly along Grosvenor Square and Hyde Park.

Nabby and I shopped. There were laces and bolts of expensive silks which were almost nonexistent now in America. The fabrics were much better than the American goods.

After eight days, in spite of all the efforts of many American friends to show us all the sights of London, Nabby and I were getting discouraged. No word had come either from John or Johnny. We were glum.

One morning we were getting ready to visit Mr. Copely. He was the artist who had painted John's picture. Suddenly Briesler burst into the room, red in the face and puffing with excitement.

"Mrs. Adams, Ma'am," he said, trying to catch his breath. "John Quincy is here!"

"Here?"

"Yes, Ma'am. Next door."

"Why is he not here?" I asked in astonishment pointing to our room.

"He stopped to have his hair done."

At my look of surprise Nabby said, "Your son wants to present his best appearance, Mother."

Before I could make a reply a young man entered the room. He was handsome with his hair well powdered. He was tall with aristocratic features and large expressive eyes. I stood staring at him. Could this be my seventeen-year-old Johnny?

"Oh, my dear Mama!" he said.

I wanted to run to him, kiss him, and hold him close to me, but he was too grown-up for such an exhibition. I kissed him on the cheek.

Nabby and Johnny were looking at each other with deep feeling shining from their eyes.

Johnny took a step forward. "I would recognize my sister anywhere," he said with admiration evident in the tone of his voice.

Nabby curtsied, lowering her eyes with shyness. Her lips were quivering with excitement. "Oh, Johnny, it's God's blessing to see you!"

A day later Johnny found a sturdy carriage that would take us to the Hague in Holland. The carriage had to be put on board a ship at Harwich, Johnny said, and would be taken off the ship at Hellevoetsluis. It would be a twenty-six hour crossing.

On the night before we were to go to Holland I began packing. Johnny had taken Nabby to the theater. I heard a heavy step in the hallway. The door flew open. John stood

in the doorway. His clothes were dusty from
travel. His wig was askew. At the sight of me
his face looked radiant.

For a moment I could not speak. It had
been more than four years since I had seen
my beloved partner.

When he swept me into his arms, the years
disappeared. All the aches and fears and
troubles left my heart.

John held my face a few inches from his.
"You haven't changed a bit, Miss Adorable,"
he said. "The very sight of you makes me feel
twenty years younger!"

My heart was so full I could not speak.

John went on, "I could not wait to see you.
I managed to get passage from Holland. We'll
go to France from here."

"Oh, John," I cried, "I am eager to begin
life again together."

The four of us reached Paris by the middle
of August. The dirt and obnoxious odors
filled my nostrils. It was necessary to keep
my handkerchief at my nose. It was best to
breathe through cologne to block out the ugly
odors.

As our coach clattered through the narrow
streets of the city, Nabby said, "I never saw
so many people in one place, even on the
Boston Common."

John Quincy laughed at his sister. "Paris is
really a beautiful city, Nabby," he said.
"Wait until you see the lovely gardens, the
theater, and the art galleries, and the ballet."

"But look," protested Nabby. "There's a
dead dog lying in the street on top of kitchen
debris! The gutters are full of garbage!"

"I have never liked the putrid streets of
Paris either," said John. "Therefore I've
leased the house of the Comte de Rouault in

Auteuil. It adjoins the Bois de Boulogne, overlooking the river Seine, and is surrounded by beautiful gardens."

The house was about four miles out of the city. It was a fine white stone mansion.

"Is it expensive?" I asked, knowing that John's salary had been cut. Congress was allowing him very little.

"If we want our country to be respected, we must live up to a standard that will command respect," John answered.

There were eight servants on the staff besides the two Breislers. This was an extravagance that was hard for me to reckon with especially since the French servants insisted on doing only the work in their own special line. There was not one who considered cleaning the stairway his work and finally Briesler had to do it.

However, the servant problem could not overshadow the good happenings. Fortunately there were some of our good friends living in Paris. Mr. Franklin lived only a mile away. Thomas Jefferson, who was to work on treaties too, had come to Paris with his daughter, Patsy. And we became close friends with the family of the Marquis de Lafayette. Madam de Lafayette, although from one of the wealthiest families in France, dressed simply and had charming manners. We saw much of each other.

John Quincy took us sight-seeing, but on Sundays I insisted we stay home.

I told John, "Pleasure seems to be the chief interest among the French, even on the Sabbath they roust about. God's words, 'Remember the sabbath day, to keep it holy' (Exodus 20:8), do not seem to apply here. We shall observe the Lord's day."

"Yes, we shall," agreed John.

Nabby soon pointed out that even the clothes we had bought in London were out of date in Paris. I heard of a little dressmaker who had been apprenticed to the queen's dressmaker. We had new silk dresses made that were as fashionable as those worn by the ladies of the court, and less costly.

As days went on, there were many official visitors at our mansion. I wished our reception room was more elegant. Extravagantly I ordered new furniture. The chairs were beautifully carved and were covered with red damask.

"Abigail," John said almost reproachfully, "are these not too expensive?"

"Yes, they are, John," I answered, "but there is nothing like them in Boston. I would like to take them home with us."

John gave me a knowing smile. "Even your Grandmother Quincy never had anything so fine," he said.

Early in 1785 Benjamin Franklin resigned and was given permission to return home. Thomas Jefferson was appointed minister to France, and John was appointed the first minister from the United States to England. My stay in France was over!

One day I asked John to walk with me. We strolled along the Seine with budding spring flowers all around us. It was a sparkling day of sunshine.

"It will be a difficult job," John was saying. "I don't know how the English will take to a minister from a nation which has just finished a war to separate from them."

"How could I have ever thought Paris was dirty," I mused. "It's a beautiful city. Let's drive up to the top of Montmartre for one last view of the city that I can carry with me forever."

"You are a romanticist," laughed John.

"Paris has made me more tolerant of other people," I said. "She has made me a citizen of the world."

"Can we, as citizens of the world, handle King George III?" John asked.

"There would be no one better able to do it," I answered, trying to give John the confidence he needed.

Secretly I was worried about how we would be received in London, but I kept my fear-filled thoughts from John.

John Quincy would not be going with us. He decided to return to the United States and study law at Harvard.

There were many farewell parties, but the most difficult farewell was with the servants who wept when we left. I was surprised at the pangs I felt at parting with the servants of whom I had become fond in the past ten months.

London was crowded at the end of May. It was King George III's birthday. John had rented a lovely house in Grosvenor Square.

When John had his first audience with King George, Nabby and I could hardly wait to hear how he was received.

"What did you say to King George?" Nabby asked.

"I said I thought myself fortunate to have the honor to be the first American to be minister to his court," replied John. "I told him, 'I hope to restore the good relations between two people who have the same language and blood.' "

The day arrived when Nabby and I were to accompany John to court to be presented to the royal family. My heart raced at the thought of meeting the king and queen. Would I be clever; would I be dull?

I asked the dressmaker to make our gowns as simple as possible. My gown was white crepe. It was trimmed with lilac ribbon and

mock point lace. The hoops beneath the skirts were bigger than I liked. The great train was much too long, but the dressmaker assured me it was necessary. I wore lace gloves and a very handsome cap from which two white plumes rose to great heights. John presented me with matching pearl earrings and necklace for the occasion.

Nabby's dress was also white crepe and was trimmed with white ribbons.

"My lands, Ma'am," Esther exclaimed, "Them long trains 'ill sweep clean all the palace floors." We laughed at Esther and she laughed too.

On the day of the presentation my hands shook visibly as we left for Buckingham Palace at one o'clock; Nabby and I in one carriage and John and a Colonel Smith, who was John's new assistant, in another.

When we arrived at the palace we were escorted to a drawing room where there were over two hundred people waiting to be presented. My heart pounded. "Would I know what to say to King George?"

King George entered. He made a circle to the right. Finally he came to me. His voice was low. I drew off my right glove. And King George III kissed my left cheek. He said: "Mrs. Adams, have you taken a walk today?"

I could not tell him that I had had no time for walks. I had spent the whole morning getting ready for this reception.

I said, "No, sire."

"Why? Don't you love walking?" asked King George.

"I am rather indolent in that respect, Your Majesty," I said.

Then King George was introduced to Nabby who bowed beautifully.

It was two more hours before Queen Charlotte decided to greet us. My silk shoes, made to match my dress, were not made for standing! My feet hurt. My back ached and I longed to go home.

Finally Queen Charlotte, the princesses, and the ladies-in-waiting made their way to us. Queen Charlotte seemed to stiffen. Her face wore a pained expression. I sensed that she was embarrassed.

"Mrs. Adams," she addressed me coolly, "have you got into your house?"

"Not yet, Your Highness," I said. "But our furniture is expected daily from The Hague."

She bowed stiffly and moved along.

I was glad the presentation was over.
Queen Charlotte had done little to hide her
dislike of Americans. In a few minutes we
were dismissed and all the plans and work
and anticipation were as nothing.

When we were home I told John, "That
woman may be the Queen, but she is no
lady!"

Chapter XI

The Vice-President's Lady

Although diplomatic life took much of my time, Nabby took her share of my time too. Young Colonel Smith, John's aide, always seemed to be where Nabby was. He made it clear that he wanted her close attention, and he was getting it. He let her know by every look that he adored her.

Soon Colonel Smith asked John's permission to marry Nabby. There was not much else to say but "yes" to Smith. He came from a good family. He was thirty years old, had been one of Washington's aides in the Revolution; he was tall and clever. John and I agreed to the match.

The Bishop of St. Asaph agreed to perform
the marriage ceremony. The Patriots admired him because he had written that he
looked up to America "as the only great
nursery of freedom now left upon the face of
the earth."

The ceremony was held in the embassy. It
was hard for me to believe I had a daughter
old enough to be married. But it was 1786,
and Nabby would soon be twenty-one.

Colonel Smith and Nabby rented a house
on Wimpole Street, not far from Grosvenor
Square and had dinner with us every day.

In December 1787 John was given permission to resign his post and return home. It
was not until April that we were ready to
leave England. By this time, the new
Constitution had been written and was being
considered for approval by the thirteen
states.

Nabby and her husband, Colonel William
Smith, did not wait to return with us.
William wanted to get to New York as
quickly as possible. He wanted to find out
what possibilities there were for him in the
new government.

We had our last audience with King
George III before we left London. He had
been agreeable to John and me.

When we came into King George's presence he greeted us warmly, saying, "Madam
and Ambassador Adams, I remember very
well my first conversation with the repre-
sentative of the new country. Mr. Adams
told me, 'I have no attachment but to my own
country,' a very admirable thing to say."

Looking at the heavy-jowled, short, plump
King of England I remembered how once
back in Weymouth I had admired him as a

Patriot King. I had quoted whole passages from one of the speeches he had given to Parliament.

King George kissed my cheek. John and I backed out of his presence and hurried down the palace steps to our waiting carriage. Tears misted my eyes. I had come to like the King of England.

Four days later we left from Portsmouth on the *Lucretia*.

"Are you sure, Abby, that you can go back to the simple life?" John asked.

"I have seen life in high positions," I answered. "But I am looking forward to returning to my little farm."

"I mean to retire to Braintree as a private citizen," John said. "I've been out of my country for ten years. I'll need time to settle in. I have no further ambition, except to live my life quietly with my family, as a farmer, and perhaps a writer of history."

But as the *Lucretia* sailed into Boston Harbor an official barge left the dock carrying the secretary of state and a committee sent by Governor John Hancock.

"A welcoming committee, John!" I exclaimed.

As we stepped off the ship two thousand Bostonians cheered us. Bells rang. There was booming of cannons. People waving hats and handkerchiefs lined the streets as our carriage, drawn by four matched bays rode to the Hancock mansion.

Slipping my hand into John's, I smiled up at my astonished husband.

"I never expected this," he whispered. "I have considered what I have done rather modest. My failures have been numerous."

As I bathed in Dorothy Hancock's five-

foot-long bathtub my mind was not on the
state dinner for fifty which the Hancocks
were giving in our honor, but rather on the
exciting emotion that we would see our sons
again!

The next day John was received in the
Representatives' Hall of the State House.
Both Houses gave him honors. John was
glowing with pleasure. But the greatest
pleasure of all was when we returned to the
Hancocks' parlor and found Charley and
Tommy waiting for us.

They were wearing spotless white shirts.
Both boys wore long hair.

I stared at my two sons unbelievingly.
Charley was now eighteen and a junior at
Harvard. He looked so much like Nabby!
Tommy was past fifteen and short and
stocky.

Holding back my desire to hug my boys
and smother them with kisses I waited until
they came to us, bowing and shaking hands in
the proper manner.

"Johnny is very well," Charley said. "After
graduating from Harvard with honors he
secured an apprenticeship with a leading
lawyer, Theophilus Parsons of Newburyport,
Massachusetts."

"Johnny will be in Boston as soon as he can
get transportation," Tommy said.

Charley relaxed a little after conversation
had begun and leaned over to me and
whispered, "We can't wait till we're all
together at home Ma."

"We are going back to Braintree," I
whispered back. "Your father will go before I
do to make everything ready. I shall wait
here in Boston for Johnny."

John left at daybreak for Braintree. At ten thirty Johnny arrived. Even though I had not seen him for three years, this time he had not changed. He was unkempt after his long ride, but still the fine erect figure he had always been.

Johnny rushed to me and taking both of my hands in his said, "Dear Mama. How good to see you, my dearest friend and counselor!"

Throwing social customs to the wind I held my son close and laid my head on his shoulder. Indeed he was my friend. I thought back to my girlhood when I had yearned for a friend. I had found John. Now I had another dear friend, my oldest son.

Johnny held me close as he said, "I have a whole month to spend with you and Papa."

Back in Braintree John spent all of his time bringing the farm up to usefulness. He hired men to clear the fields of stones, build fences, plow, and bring in hay.

One afternoon John came to the kitchen door with six Guernseys.

"What are these?" I asked.

"Cows," he said with a broad grin.

"What are we going to do with them?"

"Milk them."

"But, John," I protested, "we have no cow barn."

"I didn't consider that," said John. "I'm so anxious to be a farmer again, I just couldn't wait to get some cows."

"Johnny and I have figured our books," I said. "It has already cost us five thousand dollars to fix the house and the farm!"

"That's exactly what the government owes us in back pay," John pointed out.

By December the states were having

elections. Massachusetts chose its electors,
who would vote for the President and
Vice-President. New York was chosen as the
seat of the government.

On the first Wednesday in February 1789,
the electors of eleven states met in their
capitals to vote. They sent their ballots to
Congress in New York. George Washington
was unanimously elected President. John
was elected Vice-President only because he
had more votes than anyone else for the
office. He received only thirty-four votes,
which was less than half.

"Abigail," he said, "I am angry. I am hu-
miliated. Should I accept the vice-presidency
with so few votes?"

My eyes filled with tears, but I spoke in a
firm voice. "You have been elected," I said.
"The Constitution does not provide any other
way for us to get a Vice-President."

In New York on April 13 George Washington came to the Senate Chamber. John
formally received him and then led him to the
portico overlooking Wall and Broad Streets.
Washington bowed to the crowd below. A
great cheer went up for the war hero. He
moved forward and stood close to the iron
railing.

Samuel Otis, Secretary of the Senate,
raised the Bible from the table. Chancellor
Robert R. Livingston of New York gave the
oath of office.

After George Washington took the oath
the Chancellor said, "Long live George
Washington, President of the United
States."

It was a thunderbolt of a moment! The
people cheered. The American flag was

raised on Federal Hall. The ships in the harbor gave a thirteen-gun salute, the bells rang.

President Washington returned to the Chamber and gave his address.

But I knew the vice-presidency was not an important position. The Constitution had given him nothing to do except preside over the Senate. John would be important only if there was a great tragedy.

John rented a house for us on Richmond Hill, a mile out of the city of New York. It was a lovely place with a view of the Hudson River. To the north there were fields where cattle grazed; to the south I could see the roofs of New York.

"Like our new home?" John asked.

"Oh, yes, John," I smiled. "It's a lovely place and besides I shall have nearly all my children with me."

Nabby and her family lived in New York. Charles and Tommy would be with us. Johnny was in Boston practicing law and could make the trip frequently.

"My first official act shall be to call on Mrs. Washington," I told John.

"Yes," John nodded.

Ordering our carriage I was driven to the large house where the Washingtons lived on Cherry Street.

President Washington introduced us and then excused himself.

When I sat down to talk to Mrs. Washington, I knew instantly that I was going to like her. She was about ten years older than me. She was short and plump. Her dress was simple and she wore a cap on her shining-clean white hair.

An almost instant friendship sprang up between us.

"You have so much experience in politics, Mrs. Adams," said Martha Washington. "You must advise me what to do in this new circumstance in which I find myself. I have a fear of making mistakes."

"I have lived a great part of my life on farms in Massachusetts," I said. "The only high society I've known is European. I will tell you all I know."

Martha Washington and I became friends. We exchanged visits quite often. We went on outings together in the country, once spending three delightful days on an excursion to the Passaic in New Jersey.

Then President and Mrs. Washington moved. When the Macomb house on

Broadway was available, President Washington leased it.

That spring was cold, wet, and windy. President Washington took a severe cold. It developed into pneumonia. A fourth doctor was sent for.

The President was sinking rapidly. No one worked. News swept through New York and people wept openly.

After a visit to the Washington home, on the fifth day of the President's illness, John and I came home in despair.

I said, "I fear a thousand things which I pray I may never be called upon to experience."

John was wiping his forehead and his damp hands as he paced the room in agony. His eyes were deep purple. "We simply cannot lose George Washington," he moaned. "He makes the government work. We need him. Oh, dear Lord, spare our great leader!"

The next morning I went to the Washington home to see if I could be of some help to Martha. She came out of the President's bedchamber.

Martha crossed over to me saying softly, "I fear he is dying. There is a rattle in his throat."

I took her hands in mine. We bowed our heads. I prayed aloud, "Our Father, our Shield and our Defender, we call on Thee to spare us our great leader whom we need in these troubled times. Almighty God, we ask in Jesus' name. Amen."

Tears came to my eyes and spilled over my cheeks. I put my arms around Martha's shoulders. We stood looking at each other, words were not necessary.

When I returned home John was sitting dejectedly in his chair. He glanced up. Seeing my tear stained face, he buried his face in his hands and his shoulders heaved convulsively.

Our prayers joined with the millions of prayers that were being spoken that day. The doctors had done all they knew to do. Only God could help. In the afternoon the President's fever broke.

There was great relief and rejoicing throughout the new nation. We turned our energies again to our country.

There was a flood of visitors always at our New York home. Senators and their wives, as well as congressmen came to breakfast, dinner, and tea. Our home was a pleasant distance to ride out of the city. I was expert enough by now at mass entertaining, and enjoyed the sociability.

In one year the capital was moved to Philadelphia temporarily.

"Why Philadelphia?" I asked John.

"Because, dear Abby, the House has already voted for it. After Philadelphia we will move to a permanent site on the Potomac River. A whole new federal city will be built there. It's a horse trade."

"How, John?"

"The Southerners will vote for our tax bill if the new capital city is located in the South."

Philadelphia rented the best house in town for President Washington. He made extensive changes at his own expense.

On Tuesdays he saw congressmen and visitors from other states and from foreign lands. On Thursday nights the Washingtons always gave a dinner. On Friday evenings

Mrs. Washington entertained ladies in the drawing room from seven to nine. At all the events there was much talk of the French Revolution.

We lived at Bush Hill. The rooms were spacious. There was a fine view of the city and the surrounding flatlands.

During my second year in Philadelphia, I had a long, serious illness. It was as if my body were having conflicts of its own. A twenty-pound loss of weight had turned me from a well filled-out woman to a gaunt one. But my faith was constant and I prayed for strength.

Going home to Braintree to the part which was now called Quincy in honor of my grandfather, health flowed back into my body. I was grateful and said many times: "Unto thee, O Lord, do I lift up my soul" (Psalm 25:1).

One spring morning in 1792, George Washington and John were reelected. I received a message that revived my good spirits more than any medicine could. President Washington had appointed our Johnny as minister to Holland! An ambassador at twenty-six! But during John's second term I stayed in Quincy.

In 1793 King Louis XVI and Marie Antoinette were guillotined. Lafayette was imprisoned. When I lived in France all three of them had been kind to me, and I grieved for them.

In 1796 President Washington refused to run for another term. He thought two terms were enough for any President. John told me that Washington was eager to retire to Mount Vernon in Virginia. His farm needed

him. Besides he was not happy about the way
the newspapers wrote about him.

On February 8, 1797, my husband rode to
Independence Square and went up to the
Senate Chamber on the second floor of
Congress Hall. He called the Senate and the
House to order. Secretary of the Senate,
Samuel Otis, approached John with a locked
metal case. It contained ballots of the sixteen
states of the Union.

The tally was handed to John who stood up
and read, "The new President of the United
States is John Adams with 71 electoral votes.
The new Vice-President is Thomas Jefferson
with sixty-eight."

The United States Senate rose. They gave
John a loud ovation.

At the time when all this was happening in
Philadelphia I was sitting at John's desk in
Quincy tallying the unofficial votes as I knew

them. The results were those that John had just announced from the podium miles away. I wrote:

The sun is dressed in brightest beams
To give thy honors to the day.

Then I dropped my head, "And now, O Lord, my God, Thou hast made Thy servant ruler over the people. Give unto him an understanding heart that he may know how to go out and come in before this great people; that he may discern between good and bad . . . ."

I went on writing, "My thoughts and meditations are with you, though personally absent; and my petitions to heaven are that 'The things that make the peace may not be hidden from your eyes.' . . . with honor to yourself, with justice and impartiality to your country, and with satisfaction to this great people, shall be the daily prayer of your A.A."

CHAPTER XII

𝕱𝖎𝖗𝖘𝖙 𝕷𝖆𝖉𝖞

It was a May morning in 1797. As my carriage rattled along toward Philadelphia my thoughts were with John who was now the second President of the United States. I hadn't seen him since he had taken office in March. I was grateful that John's mother, who had passed away recently, had lived long enough to know that her son was President.

Just after my carriage passed Trenton, about twenty-five miles out of Philadelphia, I saw a carriage blocking the road. As we drew closer I glimpsed John inside!

President John Adams came to me with a broad, happy smile. I transferred to his coach. It was the happiest of meetings!

"We have so much to talk about, John," I said, holding his hands in mine as if never to let them go again.

"Let me look at you, Miss Adorable," John smiled. "I had to come to meet your coach," John said. "I felt I couldn't live without you another day!"

We stopped at an inn at Bristol. We were seated at a front window overlooking the Delaware River. As we ate an unhurried meal John confided the news to me.

"Johnny will become the minister to Prussia," he said. "It is not a promotion for Johnny, but he can do more for our country there."

"And isn't it happy news that Johnny is to marry Louisa Johnson?" I asked.

"Yes, yes," agreed John. "I enjoyed the girl when we first met her and her family in London."

I had long known that Johnny had fallen in love with Louisa in England. She was the daughter of Joshua Johnson who was the American consul in London. Louisa had been born in London.

"But what about the job of President, John?" I asked. "What problems do you see?"

"There will be many problems," said John, his eyes clouding over. "There are so many people asking for jobs! Then, there are those who didn't like my inaugural address when I said we had to deal firmly with France. Thomas Jefferson for one, is opposing my views on France."

John reached for my hand and looked deeply into my eyes saying, "Dear Abby, could you possibly know what it is like to be constantly surrounded by people and not be able to tell your real thoughts to any of them? I have never needed you more than I do now in this lonely office of the President."

"I'll always be with you, John," I told him.

We moved into the President's house, the one George Washington had vacated. It became my habit to rise at five each morning and use this quiet time for prayer. After my time with God, I wrote letters to the family, suggested menus, and read the papers John set out for me to study.

After Briesler served breakfast in the small dining room downstairs, we discussed the problems of the day. John often quoted such passages as Galatians 5:22: "But the fruit of the Spirit is love, joy, peace, longsuffering, gentleness, goodness, faith, meekness, temperance: against such there is no law." Trying to bring these qualities to daily problems helped us to find solutions.

There were receptions and dinners. John's

receptions were not as formal as George Washington's had been. President Washington was usually dressed in black velvet and did not shake hands with the people who came to his receptions. John dressed simply in a plain grey or black suit with a white ruffled collar. He shook hands with everyone and spoke cordially to people about their local politics, their families, and whatever seemed to interest them.

But John always had serious problems on his mind. We had a letter from Johnny. He wrote that Napoleon and his aides were "men without principle, and most inveterate enemies of America . . . ."

John told me his letter from John Marshall said that leaders in France had refused to see the three American commissioners and that they had been treated in an undignified manner. Publication of the insults to the American commissioners stirred the people from New York to Georgia.

The mood of the country was set for war. Congress passed twenty bills which moved America toward war with France. When Congress adjourned in the summer of 1798, John and I went back to Quincy. My health was not good. I was weary. But I took comfort in the words of Colossians 2:6 "As ye have therefore received Christ Jesus the Lord, so walk ye in him." John ran the government through correspondence with his Cabinet.

"There is talk," John told me, "that the French will invade the United States."

In the fall, when back in Philadelphia government officials began arriving at six in the morning. Even at midnight John was having conferences. As I looked at these men, filling almost all our available rooms, using all our furniture, I began to understand why Martha Washington had to replace her furniture three times.

The French seized many American ships that were trading with England. Americans were furious with France. But John worked hard and was able to make a settlement with France. War was avoided.

"If there is one statement I would like on my tombstone," said John, "it would be 'He made peace with France.' "

When Congress finished work that spring, I prepared to return to Quincy before John. On my way home I stopped in New York to see Charles. He lived near the water front. There was the harsh sound of shipping all around his house. Sounds of wheels and loadings and unloadings and men calling directions to each other echoed in the streets.

Sally, Charley's wife opened the door. She was a pretty girl with heavy-lidded eyes and a red, full mouth.

"I'm so glad to see you, Mother Adams!" she said. But her eyes were troubled.

Charley rushed to me and took both my hands in his and raised them to his lips. He was thin. His eyes were red. His mouth twitched on the left side.

"Oh, my poor Charley!" I said to myself. I felt agony, sorrow, and despair. What has happened to my handsome, laughing, self-assured boy? I tried not to show my feelings and when Charley left us to post a letter I turned to Sally.

"Sally," I said softly, "I don't mean to pry, but I love my son and if he needs help . . . "

"Yes," Sally nodded, lowering her eyes sadly, "Charley needs help. It's his conscience."

"Do you want to tell me about it?" I patted her hand sympathetically.

"It started when John Quincy sent Charley part of his salary to invest for him. Charley made a poor investment and has lost his brother's money. He turned to drinking too much."

I left with a heavy heart. "Oh dear God, no," my thoughts cried out, "don't let Charley destroy himself!" I wept. At twenty-nine Charles was a sick and dying man. I prayed God would help him.

By November it was clear that the election of 1800 was getting under way. The visitors who came talked of nothing else. The newspapers wrote columns about it. John did not think he would win a second term because so many congressmen disagreed with him.

Then George Washington's death on December 14 united the nation and politics were forgotten for the period of mourning. Bells rang muffled for days. There were funeral processions with citizens wearing crepe bands around their arms. There were many orations and ceremonial services for the much beloved Washington.

Tommy was living with us. His problem wasn't a lack of law business, but it was avoiding that business which might come to him because he was the President's son. One day he invited twenty-eight young unmarried ladies and gentlemen to dinner. As I rose from the table Tommy helped me with my chair and leaning over whispered into my ear, "Do you have any objection to my having a party this evening?"

"No," I smiled.

John came to watch the young people for about an hour. I stayed to chaperone the party.

At midnight, when the last guest left, Tommy took my arm and walked upstairs with me. He was flushed and happy.

"That was nice of you, Mother," he smiled down at me. "I enjoyed the Philadelphia belles!"

I glanced at him. Tommy had grown up.

Congress passed the resolution that they would meet in Washington City on the third Monday of November 1800. For almost ten years designers and workmen had been working in what was to be the new capitol, Washington City, in what had been named the District of Columbia.

At first John wasn't too much in favor of moving the capitol, but he changed his mind. He said, "In a certain sense it will make us a full-fledged nation. It is appropriate because it is carved out of the wilderness as was this nation. I'm proud that I will be the first President to hold office there."

Congress passed a bill to give fifteen thousand dollars to the President to furnish his home.

"We will have to be careful buyers," I told John. "We were given fourteen thousand to furnish the Philadelphia house, and the house in Washington must be at least four times as big as this one."

I gave my last Philadelphia drawing room reception for two hundred friends and government people.

The trip to the new capital would be a difficult one. I had been warned of that. But I had not realized that the trip would plunge us deeper and deeper into the woods. Susan, Charles' four-year-old daughter who was with me, began to cry.

Finally I called out, "We're lost!"

The road was nothing more than two tracks through a thick forest. The coachman stopped and broke off branches so that our coach could get through. A woodcutter came from the depth of the forest and helped him.

All along the way I tried to cheer myself by picturing the great home that was waiting for us. I had seen the drawing and the plans of the elegant mansion with its sweeping lawns and could hardly wait to get there.

It was one o'clock when we arrived at the new President's mansion. At first sight of it I cried, "It's lovely!"

There stood a large building of white sandstone gleaming in the November sun.

But it looked bare and cold. There were no
fences, or lawns, or gardens or walks. Shacks
of the workers were all around and there
were the pits of abandoned brick kilns.

Then I saw John standing on the wooden
steps. He was smiling. Our two nephews
Billy Cranch and Billy Shaw were with John.
In back of the three men I recognized
Briesler, Betsy and Becky (the two maids I
had sent ahead), and Shipley and Richard,
two helpers from Quincy.

After happy greetings John took my arm
and led me through the front door saying,
"Mrs. Adams, welcome to the President's
mansion."

Looking about eagerly I let out a gasp. The
entrance was bare to the studdings, the
stairway wasn't in, most of the first floor
hadn't even been plastered yet.

"You'll find things more cozy upstairs,"
John hastened to say.

The Oval Room was finished. Two bed-
rooms were in good condition, especially the
little one for Susan where there was even
paint on the walls.

The next day, as Briesler was trying to
start a fire in one of the fireplaces Betsy came
to me, her forehead wrinkled into a frown.
"Mrs. Adams," she said, "we got a problem."

"Yes, we do," I agreed, looking at the
stubborn fire.

"No Ma'am, what I mean is, I done the
washing. We washed in tubs in the kitchen.
And now the washing is laying in baskets
with da water running out of it. And there's
no place to hang it up. There's no line up,"
Betsy stopped talking to take a deep breath.

"We'll find a place," I smiled at the girl.

Betsy and I looked into several half-finished rooms and finally opened the door of an immense room on the east side of the building. This room was to be used as an audience chamber. It was to be called "The East Room."

"This room is big enough for a meeting-house," Betsy said staring wide-eyed.

"Then there's plenty of room for our laundry," I told Betsy. I let out a giggle as Betsy hurried for a clothesline.

There was a knock on the door and Briesler came to me saying that Martha Washington had sent a note. "Mrs. Washington sent some venison, Mrs. Adams, and sent this note for you."

It was an invitation to visit Mount Vernon which was a short drive away. Mrs. Washington's friendship warmed my heart and the day grew more cheerful.

Election time was drawing near. It was not certain that John would win a second term. As usual my thoughts turned to Scripture. "The Lord is my strength and song, and is become my salvation" (Psalm 118:14). "Cast thy burden upon the Lord, and he shall sustain thee" (Psalm 55:22).

It was the strength of the Scripture that sustained me when John got the news that he had lost the election and that Thomas Jefferson was the new President.

At the news John buried his head in his hands. "I wanted four more years to prove our country can grow. I wanted to be part of this new capital city." John's voice sounded hoarse and his eyes were moody purple.

I crossed the Oval Room and sat beside my husband.

"We wanted to serve. We have served. There is now a nation called the United States. Your courage and your vision have brought the people of this great nation a long way from the injustices of the Stamp Act. With God's help you have been an important part in building the freest nation the world has ever known."

A sparkle came into John's eyes. He held out both arms to me. "Thank you, Miss Adorable," he said, "for all the wonderful gifts of life you have brought me over the years."

"And now we shall begin a new life together in Quincy," I told my dearly beloved John.

BIBLIOGRAPHY

Bailey, Carolyn Sherwin. *Tell Me A Birthday Story*. (New York: Stokes Co., 1935).

Bobbe, Dorothie. *Abigail Adams*. (New York: G.P. Putnam's Sons, 1966).

Chandler, Anna Curtis. *Famous Mothers and Their Children*. (New York: Fredrick A. Stokes Co., 1938).

Clarke, Fred G. *John Quincy Adams*. (New York: Collier Books, 1966).

Daugherty, Sonia. *Ten Brave Women*. (Philadelphia and New York: J. B. Lippincott Company Publ., 1953).

Fisher, Dorothy Canfield. *Our Independence and the Constitution*. (New York: Random House, 1950).

Holberg, Ruth Langland. *Abigail Adams*. (New York: Row, Peterson, 1950).

Johnson, William J. *George Washington The Christian*. (New York: Abingdon, 1919).

Kane, Joseph Nathan. *Facts About the Presidents*. (H. W. Wilson Co., 1959).

Kelly, Regina Z. *Abigail Adams: The President's Lady*. (Boston: Houghton Mifflin Co., 1962).

Lawson, Don. *Young People in the White House*. (New York: Abelard-Schuman, 1961).

Lengyel, Cornel Adam. *Presidents of the United States*. (Bantam Books, 1961).

Lomask, Milton. *John Quincy Adams*. (New York: Farrar, Straus and Giroux, 1965).

Ross, George E. *Know Your Presidents and Their Wives*. (Rand McNally & Co., 1960).

Steinberg, Alfred. *John Adams*. (New York: G. P. Putnam Sons, 1969).

Tugwell, Rexford G. *How They Became President*. (Simon & Schuster, 1964).

INDEX

A

Abby, see Abigail Adams

Active, 104-105, 108

Adams, Abigail, childhood, 1-29; youth, 30-55; courting, 56-61; engagement, 62-68; marriage, 66-71; children, 72-73; Boston, 74-80; Braintree, 81; tea party, 82-84; Braintree return, 85-91; Bunker Hill, 92-94; War, 95-103; sailing, 104-108; London, 109; Paris, 110-112; England, 113-118; Boston, 119-120; farm, 121; vice-president's lady, 122-127; First Lady, 128-140

Adams, Charles, 81, 98, 100, 103-104, 120-123, 133-134, 136

Adams, John, meeting, 38, 40-42, 46-47, 55-61; engagement, 62-67; marriage, 68-71; children, 72-73; Boston, 74-75, 77-78; trial, 79-81; tea party, 82-84; Braintree, 85; Congress, 86-100; France, 101-104; London, 108-109; Paris, 110-112; England, 113-118; Boston, 119; farm, 120-121; Vice-president, 122-123, 125-127; President, 128-140

Adams, John Quincy, 73, 77, 89, 92-94, 98-103, 108-109, 111, 113, 120-121, 123, 127, 130-131, 134

Adams, Samuel, 56, 74-75, 83-84, 86

Adams, Susan, 136

Adams, Susannah, 76

Adams, Thomas, 81, 97, 98, 100, 104, 120, 134-135

Adorable, Miss, 68, 110, 130, 140

Amherst, Lord Jeffrey, 40, 42-43, 46, 48

Anne, Aunt, 5, 8

B

baptismal, 13-14, 72

Beacon Hill, 46, 75

Betsey, 24, 104

Bible, 30, 53, 87, 98, 122

blacksmith, 18-20

Boston, 15, 19, 33-34, 40-43, 45, 49-50, 67-68, 71, 74-77, 79, 81, 83-88, 91-96, 99, 101-102, 105, 119-120

Boston Massacre, 78-79

Boston Tea Party, 82-84

Braintree, 32, 34, 37-38, 56, 64, 71, 74, 76, 81, 88, 103-104, 119-121

Breed's Hill, 92-93

Briesler, Esther, 104-106, 111, 114

Briesler, John, 104, 106, 108-109, 111, 131, 137

British, 73-75, 79, 87-89, 91, 93, 96, 102

Bunker Hill, battle, 92-94

C

Charlotte, queen, 114-116

Christian, 7, 36, 59

Common, 76, 110

Concord, 87

Congress, 86, 91, 94, 100, 103, 111, 122, 128

Constitution, 118, 123

Cranch, Richard, 54-55, 58, 61, 66, 69

D

Dame's School, 6, 42

Dartmouth, 81-83

Declaration of Independence, 98

dysentery, 97

E

Ecclesiastes, 2

Elihu, 71, 97
Elizabeth, Aunt, 5, 8, 33, 46-47
England, 36, 40-41, 48-49, 53, 58, 72, 85, 105,
    107, 112, 118

F
father, 2-7, 9, 13-14, 16-32, 56, 58, 62-65, 70,
    72
fire, 22-29
foot warmer, 25-29
France, 99-101, 131-133
Franklin, Benjamin, 99, 111-112
French, 7, 18-19, 40-41, 46, 48

G
Gage, General, Royal Governor, 85, 87
Galatians, 131
garret, 17-18, 21-22
George, II, king, 7, 72; III, 72, 88, 113-115,
    118
ghost, 21-22
God, 20, 30, 35-36, 52, 59, 64, 69, 76, 88, 90,
    97-98, 100, 109, 111, 129, 131, 134
Griffins Wharf, 79-83
Grosvenor Square, 108, 113, 118
gunpowder, 18-20, 22, 24

H
Hancock, Dorothy, 119
Hancock, John, 38, 40, 75, 119
Harvard, 38, 40, 56, 59, 113, 120
Holland, 109, 127
Hutchinson, Governor, 82, 85
Hutchinson, Stingy, Tommy, 79

I
Indian, 1, 8, 10-13, 18-19, 41, 46, 84
Isaac, Uncle, 43-46, 48-50, 105-106

J
James, 82, 102
Jefferson, Thomas, 111-112, 128, 131, 139
Jesus, 54, 93, 132
Johnson, Louisa, 130-131
Jonah, 77, 83-84

K
King Street, 77-78

L
Lexington, 87
London, 108, 118
Long Wharf, 44
Lord, 50, 69, 72-73, 77, 83, 125, 129
Lucy, Aunt, 67
Luke, 65

M
Mary, 1-2, 4, 6, 8-10, 14, 16-19, 22, 24-25,
    31-34, 54-55, 58-60, 63, 65-66, 72
Massachusetts, 2, 17, 25, 66, 69, 72-74, 86,
    120, 124
Mary, Aunt, 5, 8-10
Matthew, 34
meetinghouse, 9, 12-13, 16-18, 22-24, 27-29,
    89
minutemen, 87
mother, 2-7, 9-11, 16-17, 19-20, 24-25, 27,
    30-36, 58-59, 62-63, 66, 68-69
Mount Vernon, 127, 139
Mount Wollaston, 1-2, 34-36, 53-54, 72, 102
Mummentaug, Chief, 11

N
Nabby, 3, 5, 7, 14, 18-19, 31-35, 37, 39, 58, 64
Nabby, daughter, 72, 77, 90, 92, 98, 101,
    104-106, 108-109, 112-115, 117-118, 120, 123

Napoleon, 132
New York, 96, 99, 118, 122-123, 126, 132

O
Otis, Samuel, 122, 128

P
Paris, 110-113
Parliament, 72, 75, 119
Patriots, 88, 90, 118
Patty, 88-90, 97
Penn's Hill, 71, 92-94, 102
Peter, 71
pewter, 69, 90-91
Philadelphia, 86, 88, 94-95, 99, 126-128, 130,
    132, 135
Phoebe, 2, 4, 7, 17, 19, 30, 58, 64-65

Q
Queen Street, 81
Quincy, 127, 132, 137, 140
Quincy, Dorothy, 38, 40
Quincy, Grandfather, Colonel John, 2, 6, 8,.
    10-11, 15, 18, 34-35, 40-50, 53-54, 77
Quincy, Grandmother, 1-14, 32-39, 41-42,
    47-48, 51-55, 72
Quincy, Josiah, 79

R
Rainsford Island, 59
Revere, Paul, 5, 47-48, 87
Romans, 97
Rover, 20-22
Russia, 103

S
sampler, 33, 35-36
Savior, 52, 82

sexton, 17, 21-22
Simpson, Mr., Mrs., 25-29, 32
smallpox, 67-68, 97
Smith, Colonel, 115, 117-118
Smith, Reverend, William, see father
Smith, Will, cousin, 82
Sons of Liberty, 77
Stamp Act, 72-73, 140
Sugar Act, 69

T
tithing man, 26-27
Tittle, Mrs., 52-53
Tom, 2, 12, 32, 34, 36, 64-65
tomahawk, 1, 13, 72
Townshend Act, 75, 81
Trowbridge, Mr., 26-28
Tufts, Dr. Cotton, 56, 61-62, 65, 67
Tory, 79

V
Vice-president, 122-123, 128

W
Washington City, 135
Washington, George, 94-96, 100, 112-117,
    122-127, 131-132, 134
Washington, Martha, 123-127, 133, 139
Weymouth, 2, 6, 8, 12, 15, 17-18, 29-31, 44,
    58, 61, 64-65, 89
Whigs, 81
Will, 2-4, 16-17, 19, 24
Writs of Assistance, 56

The TOWN of BOSTON

IN

New England

by

Capt John Bonner

1722

Ætatis Suæ 60.

Engraved from a copy in the possession of Wm Taylor Esq.
and published by
GEORGE G. SMITH. ENGRAVER
1867 No 51 Washington opposite State Street Boston.
1835.

I have examined this plan and find it a copy of the original Boston July 2 1835 —

West Hill

Roxbury Flatts

Fox Hill

Beacon Hill

PowderHouse

WatchHouse

COMMON

Garden

School

Marlbro

Orange Str

Pond

Coals
Garden

Ramford

Summer Str

From Town H.
One Mile

Orange Str

Fortification

Gibbins S Yd

Scale of ¼ a Mile.

HillsWharf

Cow L

Wind Mill Point

Darby W.

Bull W.

BOSTON. N.E

Planted An. Dom. 1630

	EXPLANATION.	
A. The Old Church	1630	a. Town House.
B. Old North	1650	b. Governours House.
C. Old South	1660	c. South Gramar School.
D. Annabaptist	1680	d. North Gramar School.
E. Chh of England	1688	e. Writing School.
F. Brattle St Church	1699	f. Writing School.
G. Quakers	1710	g. Alms House.
H. New North	1714	h. Bridewell
I. New South	1716	Streets 42 Lanes 36 Alleys 22
K. French	1716	Houses near 3000.
L. New N° Brick	1721	1000 Brick rest Timber.
		Near 12000 People.

Great Fires.	
First	1653
Second	1676
Third	1679
Fourth	1683
Fifth	1690
Sixth	1691
Seventh	1702
Eigth	1711

Gen^{ll} Small Pox.	
First	1649
Second	1660
Third	1677
	1678
Fourth	1690
Fifth	1702
Sixth	1721

Engraven and Printed

Bartons Point

Copper Works

Rope Walk

Rope Walk

Lees Ship Yard

Charles River

Ferry to Charles Town

Eb N. Mill Damm

N. Water Mill

Lees Ship Yd

Huffons Point

Hunt & Whites Ship Yd

Ferry Way

Burying Place

Mill Pond.

Water Mill

Baptist Meeting

Bakers

Bucks W.

Ship Y.

Hanover St

Beling Green

Back Street

Old Way

Salem Street

North Street

Ship Street

Hanover St

Middle Street

Fish Street

Thorntons Yard

mount St

Cornhill

Union

Swallworths Wharf

Burells W.

Scottleys W.

Middflone W.

Ship Street

N.Battery

Greene &

Greenwood

Clarks Ship Yd & Wharfe

Middletons W.

Scarletts Wharfe.

Hellows Wharf

Lees Ship Yd

Long Wharfe

Old Wharfe.

Clarks Wharfe

King

Fools Wharf

Olivers Dock

Parsmens W.

Greenleafs yd

Longwater

Wings Shyd

Olivers Wharfe

Gales Ship Yd

Old Wharfe

HARBOUR

Fort Hill

S Battery.

Hubbards W.

Boſton N E. 1722.   Sold by Capt. John Bonner and Willm Price againſt ẏ Town Houſe where may be had all ſorts of Prints Mapps &c.

LIBRARY OF WORLD HEROES

Inspirational Books for Young Readers

Christopher Columbus, by Bennie Rhodes. An exciting book about a Christian explorer who sought to discover new lands to spread the gospel at the risk of shipwreck, disease, and personal failure.
Cloth, $7.95; paper, $4.95

Robert E. Lee, by Lee Roddy. A Christian of impeccable character, Lee became one of the most respected men in America—even in the face of defeat.
Cloth, $7.95; paper, $4.95

Abigail Adams, by Evelyn Witter. The story of the wife of America's second President whose personal faith in Christ kept her strong in a young war torn nation.
Cloth, $7.95; paper, $4.95

George Washington, by Norma Cournow Camp. The story of the first President who was not a great preacher or Bible scholar, but who patterned his own life around the Bible lessons he studied daily. He was a sower of seeds of faith and courage.
Cloth, $7.95; paper, $4.95

Johannes Kepler, by John Hudson Tiner. This giant of faith and science considered his scientific studies to be another way of looking into God's creation.
Cloth, $7.95; paper, $4.95

Isaac Newton, by John Hudson Tiner. Here is the life story of the astronomer and mathematician who discovered the law of gravity and who was a devout, Bible-believing Christian.
Cloth, $7.95; paper, $4.95

Abraham Lincoln, by David J. Collins. A true sower of faith and freedom, this biography describes Abe's experiences in his search for an understanding of God.
Cloth, $7.95; paper, $4.95

George Washington Carver, by David J. Collins. Read the astounding story of one man's rise from slavery and the struggles and triumphs of his faith.
Cloth, $7.95; paper, $4.95

Francis Scott Key, by David J. Collins. Loyal American patriot, preacher of God's Word, writer of our National Anthem, Rev. Francis Scott Key's life was full of challenges . . . learn of how God cares for His own.
Cloth, $7.95; paper, $4.95.

Teach Them Diligently, A Devotional Guide for Teachers Who Care, by Arthur Nazigian. Presents concisely many ways to identify the blessings of God in your educational ministry. You will be blessed each time you meditate through the book. Paper, 111 pages, **2.95**

Teacher's Report Card, by Mary Vandermey. A collection of short, warming and insightful vignettes about children and real teachers. Each chapter provides the reader with encouragement and inspiration from the Scriptures. Paper, 146 pages, $2.50 **NOW $1.00**

Bible Calculator Word Games, by Bennie Rhodes. A collection of fictitious stories based on Bible names and characters which are arithmetic problems designed for use with a pocket calculator. For children ages 9–12, it is excellent for extra-time classroom use. Paper, 160 pages, **$2.95**

FACS–Fundamentals for American Christians, by Russ Walton, Basic Biblical principles of government that should be fundamentals for American Christians. Paper, 372 pages, **NOW $3.50**

Available from your local Christian bookstore or from

Mott Media

Milford, MI 48042 / (313) 685-8773